Red Flower

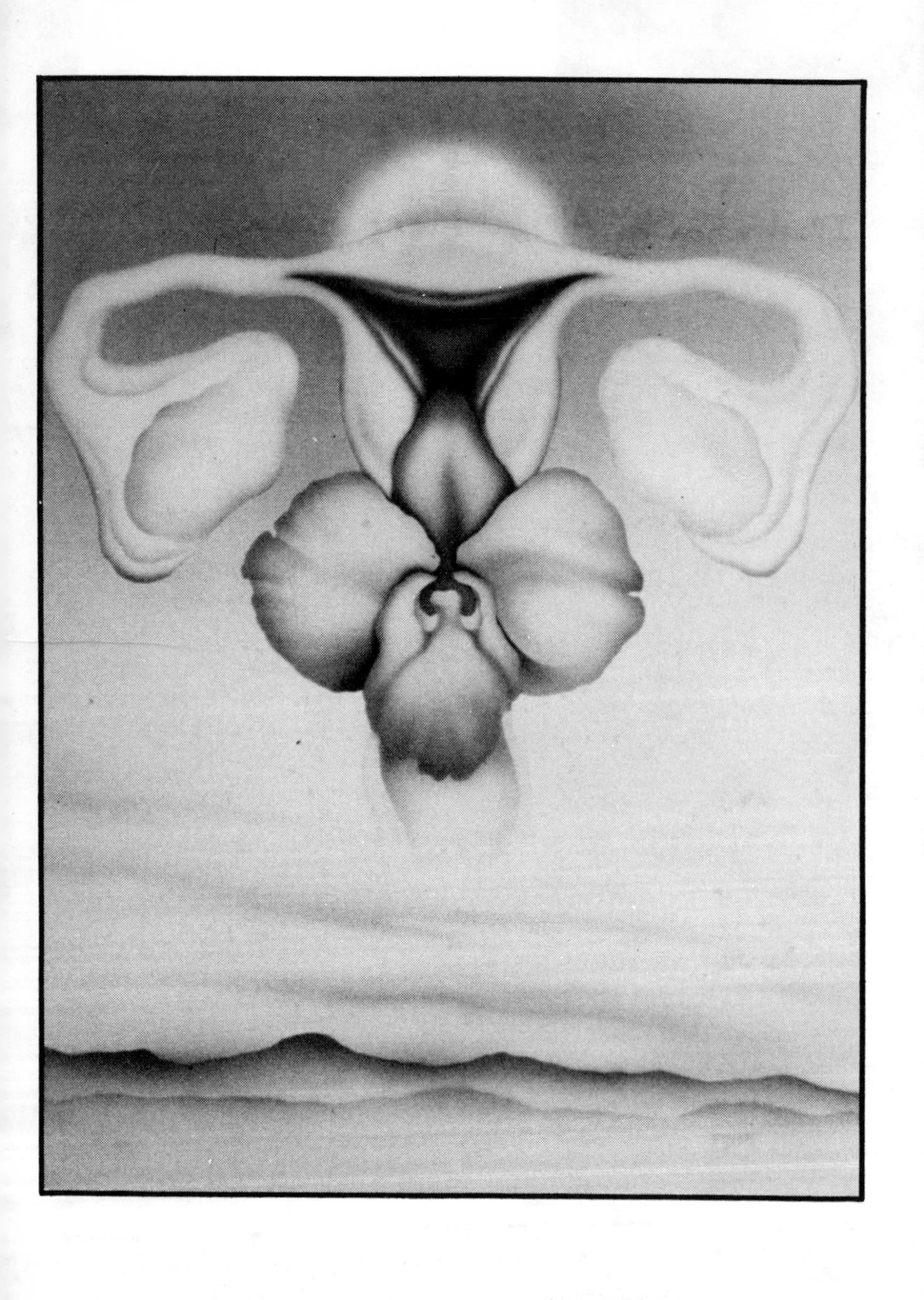

Red Flower

Rethinking Menstruation

by Dena Taylor

The Crossing Press
Freedom, California 95019

To my daughters Becky and Anna
my mother Anne
and women everywhere

Cover illustration and design by Betsy Bayley
Well Woman Series edited by Margot Edwards
Printed in the U.S.A.

Illustration opposite title page: "Fleur de Vie" by Alexia Markarian
Illustration on p. 13: "Apache mask" by Carolyn Berry
Illustration on pp. 22: "Menarche Ritual" by Jennifer Weston
Illustration on p. 29: "Detail of Aztec Painting" by Carolyn Berry
Illustration on p. 54: "Another Mystery," Subconscious Comics by Tim Eagan

Library of Congress Cataloging-in-Publication Data

Taylor, Dena.
Red flower: rethinking menstruation.

Bibliography: p.
1. Menstruation. 2. Menstruation—Miscellanea.
I. Title. II. Series.
QP263.T39 1988 612′.662 88-25673
ISBN 0-89594-313-1
ISNB 0-89594-312-3 (pbk.)

ACKNOWLEDGEMENTS

My first thanks go to Becky and Anna for their never-ending patience and help, particularly to Becky for her assistance in explaining and programming the computer and to Anna for all the lovely things she did to cheer me on. There were many times when these two teenagers gave me the encouragement I needed to push on with this book.

I will always be grateful to my friends for their tremendous support, in reading and criticizing the manuscript, cooking meals, answering questions, loaning money, bringing flowers, showing me books and articles, and encouraging me in every possible way.

Thanks also to the Santa Cruz County Library Reference Department for answering a hundred questions, and to the staff at Barnard's Center for Research on Women in New York City where I did some of the research for this book.

Special thanks go to the women who sent me poems, stories, art work, and letters of encouragement, to those who filled out the questionnaire, and those who talked with me about their menstruation experiences. This book would never have been put together without them.

I gratefully acknowledge permission from the following individuals whose work is included in the book:

Aalfs, Janet, "Rosie"
Abbott, Deborah S., "Period Poem"
Berry, Carolyn, "Indian Women & Menstruation"
Beurkens, Beth, "Rituals for Menarche"
Carter, Nancy Corson, "Menses"
Cohen, Arleen, "Each Month"
Edelson, Mary Beth, "Menstruation Stories"
Eidus, Janice, "My Valentine"
Fishman, Charles, "Blood Knowing"
Frei, Claudia, "Blood Dream"
German, Norman, "Request"
Gordon, Bonnie, "If Well Built for Sustained Assault"
Handrich, Patricia, "The Goddess and St. Valentine"
Henderson, Doris, "Last Quarter"
Kemp, Penny
Kerlikowske, Elizabeth, "I Can't—Aunt Madge is Here from Baton Rouge"
Koeppel, Mary Sue, "Wedding 1929"
Larges, Lisa, "A Menstruation Poem"
Leone, Lynn, "PMS"
Medicine Eagle, Brooke, "Grandmother Lodge"
Mott, Elaine, "Moons & Blood"
O'Dell, Mary Ernestine, "And Again"

Porter, Ginger, "Menstrual Medication"
Ptak, Carol Stone, "Menstrual Blood"
Safir, Natalie, "Misnomers"
Skelly, Margie, "Menstruation"
Sumrall, Amber Coverdale, "Twelfth Summer"
Winston, Phyllis, "The White Pad"
Zabytko, Irene, "The Women of Perm Camp—80"

I gratefully acknowledge permission from the copyright owners to reprint the following or excerpts from the following:

"A Period of Quiet But Colourful Protest," by Joan Fern Shaw, in *Fireweed,* Sept. 1985.
"A Poem of Welcome," by Judith W. Steinbergh, in *Motherwriter* by Judith W. Steinbergh, Wampeter Press, 1983.
"Bleeding to Death," by Sherry Lee, revised version; in A *Little Mixed Up,* Guild Press, 1982.
"Blood Loosens its Strangle-Hold," by Margaret Randall, in *Conditions* magazine and *Memory Speaks* by Margaret Randall, Curbstone Press, Willimantic, Connecticut, Jan. 1988.
"Celebrating the Blood: Indian Women & Menstruation," by Carolyn Berry, in *Bread & Roses,* Vol. 3, No. 3, 1984.
"Dardenella," by Dorothy Rose, in *Broomstick,* April 1980, titled "The Gate of Life Closes."
"Early Morning Love Poem," by Katharyn Machan Aal, in *SisterSource,* 1, No. 2, Sept. 1981.
Earthwalk by Philip Slater, Doubleday & Co., p. 155.
Emerging from the Chrysalis by Bruce Lincoln, Harvard Univ. Press, pp. 106-7.
"Female Blood—Roots of Shamanism," by Vicki Noble, *Shaman's Drum,* Spring 1986, p. 18.
"From Sacred Blood to the Curse and Beyond," by Judy Grahn, in *The Politics of Women's Spirituality,* ed. Charlene Spretnak, Anchor Press, pp. 266-9, 273, 275-8.
"Honoring Our Passage," by Joan B. Forest, in *Matrix,* Dec. 1986.
Hot Flashes by Barbara Raskin, St. Martin's Press, pp. 2-3.
Hygieia by Jeannine Parvati, Freestone Publishing Co., pp. 10, 13-15.
"Levi-Strauss and the Dragon: Mythologiques Reconsidered in the Light of an Australian Aboriginal Myth," by Chris Knight, in *Man,* Vol. 18, 1983, Royal Anthropological Institute of Great Britain & Ireland, p. 28.
"Lily at Twelve," by Hilary Tham, in *Paper Boats* by Hilary Tham, Three Continents Press, Urbana, IL, 1987.
Living My Life, Vol. 1, by Emma Goldman, Dover Press, p. 21.
"Mainstream, The," by Barbara Crooker, in *The Whole Birth Catalog,* Crossing Press, 1983.
Menopause—A Positive Approach by Rosetta Reitz, Penguin,

pp. 4, 67, 107, 114, 159.
"Menses," by Robert Gibb, in *Stone Country* magazine.
"Menstrual Journal," by Miriam Sagan, in *Womanspirit* magazine.
"Menstruation and Shamanism," by Marilyn Nagy in *Betwixt & Between: Patterns of Masculine and Feminine Initiation,* ed. Mahdi, et al., Open Court Publishers, La Salle, IL, p. 23.
"Menstruation and the power of Yurok women: methods of cultural reconstruction," by Thomas Buckley, *American Ethnologist,* No. 9.
Not for Innocent Ears, by Ruby Modesto and Guy Mount, Sweetlight Books, Box 307, Arcata, CA, p. 42.
"Red as Blood," by Karen Loeb, in *Sunbury,* #6.
"Removing Stains," by Nancy Shiffrin, in *What She Could Not Name,* La Jolla Poets' Press, La Jolla, CA, 1987.
"Rust," by Kathryn Kerr, in *First Frost* by Kathryn Kerr, Storm Line Press, Urbana, IL, 1985.
"Sacrament," by Janet Ruth Heller, copyright 1976 by *WomanSpirit.*
Sassafrass, Cypress & Indigo by Ntozake Shange, St. Martin's Press, pp. 19-21.
"Something to look forward to," by Marge Piercy, reprinted by permission of Middlemarch, Inc., copyright 1988 by Alfred A. Knopf, Inc.
"Tampons," by Ellen Bass, in *Our Stunning Harvest,* New Society Publishers, 1985.
"Variations in Red," by Marion Cohen, in *A Voyage Out.*
Wise Wound, The by Penelope Shuttle & Peter Redgrove, Grove Press, pp. 33, 41, 58, 79, 89, 97, 184, 218.
Women's Encyclopedia of Myths & Secrets by Barbara G. Walker, Harper & Row, pp. 638, 641.
"Women's Moontime—A Call to Power," by Brook Medicine Eagle, in *Shaman's Drum,* Spring 1986, p. 21.

I gratefully acknowledge the following artists for permission to publish their work:

Berry, Carolyn, "Apache Mask" and "Detail of Aztec painting"
Eagan, Tim, "Another Mystery"
Markarian, Alexia, "Fleur de Vie"
Weston, Jennifer, "Menarche Ritual"

pp. [illegible] 15

"[illegible]," by Robert Gibb, in *Yoga Journal* magazine.

"Menstrual Journal," by Miriam [illegible], in *[illegible]* magazine.

"Menstruation and [illegible]," by Marilyn Nasy, in *[illegible]*, [illegible] Press, [illegible] Meth[illegible], Green Crone Publishers, [illegible], pp. 23.

"Menstruation and the power of women: [illegible] methods of cultural [illegible] dissemination," by Thomas Buckley, *[illegible] Ethnologist*, No. [illegible]

Not [illegible] [illegible] by Kathy [illegible] and [illegible], [illegible] Box [illegible], Arcata, Ca. [illegible]

"[illegible] is Blood," [illegible]

"Removing Stains," by Nancy Shelton, in *[illegible] the Coming Of Age*, Little Poets Press, [illegible] 1987.

"[illegible]," by Kathryn [illegible], Stone [illegible] Press, [illegible] 1982.

"[illegible]," by Jane [illegible] Heller, copyright 1976 by [illegible].

[illegible] Cypress & [illegible] by [illegible] Sherr, St. Martin's Press, [illegible] 1991.

"Something [illegible] forward to," by [illegible], reprinted by [illegible] of [illegible], copyright 19[illegible] by Alfred A. Knopf, Inc.

"[illegible]," by [illegible], in *Our [illegible] Harvest*, New Society Publishers, 198[illegible]

"Variations in Red," by Marion Cohen, in *[illegible] Out*.

The Wound, The by Penelope Shuttle & Peter Redgrove, Grove Press, pp. 13, [illegible] 38, 79, [illegible] 1986.

Woman's Encyclopedia of Myths & Secrets by Barbara G. Walker, Harper & Row, pp. 635, 641.

"Women's [illegible] in [illegible]," by [illegible] Medicine Eagle, in *[illegible]*, Spring, 19[illegible], p. 21.

Table of Contents

Table of Contents

The true magic of menstruation is that it arouses one's passions and creativity. *The Wise Wound*

Introduction

The inspiration for this book came in a Women's Studies class at Cabrillo Community College in Aptos, California. The instructor, Beth Beurkens, introduced us to readings by Native American women which described menstruation as a sacred, powerful event. An outpouring of menstruation stories followed—some spoken for the first time—that told of shame, distress and misery, contrasting sharply with the positive feelings of the Native American women.

My own experience with the menstrual cycle was rather neutral, neither celebrated nor shameful, and my curiosity was piqued by the fact that menstruation could be experienced in such profoundly different ways. I was disturbed by the negative comments of the women in the class, and began talking to women everywhere about their feelings on menstruation. I decided to write about it, emphasizing the positive and celebratory aspects. I solicited various publications for poems, stories and art work about menstruation and the response was enthusiastic. Many letters accompanied the material that came in, full of encouragement for a book such as this.

This led me to research other cultures' menstrual practices and attitudes. I also drew up a questionnaire which elicited personal accounts from women in the United States about various aspects of menstruation. Many of the comments from the questionnaire are integrated into the text.

My goal is to show that women *do* celebrate and honor menstruation. I want to help dispel the idea that menstruation is shameful, that it should be kept hidden. We need to recognize this part of our cycle—to be aware of its subtle and powerful effects on us, and to use these in a way that enriches our lives.

The title '*Red Flower*' is taken partly from a family tradition. "Flower" has been our name for vagina ever since my daughters were tiny. I first heard it from a friend who told me that when she admonished her two-year-old once for touching herself in public, her daughter shot back defiantly: "It's *my* flower!" So flower it is, and a red flower, then, is a menstrual one.

As a verb, 'to flower,' according to the Oxford English Dictionary, means "to bloom or blossom...to expand, open." A lovely image of menstruation, bringing to mind not only a young woman's flowering into womanhood at her menarche, but also the openness, the sensitivity, the creativity which comes to women of all ages at the time of bleeding. Judy Grahn has said: "Menstruation is the flower of a woman, the bloom of her potential..."[1]

And a flower, as in flow-er, or that which flows, is what we are when we menstruate.

Menstrual blood itself has been called "the flowers," and is often associated with flowers. One of the OED's definitions of "flowers" is "the menstrual discharge; the menses," and includes this quote from the year 1662: "It helpeth the stopping of the Flowers." But, says that dictionary, this meaning of "flowers" has "fallen into disuse."

The Bible (Leviticus 15:24) also refers to menstrual blood as the flower which must come before the "fruit," or child. And *The Women's Encyclopedia of Myths and Secrets* says, "As any flower mysteriously contained its future fruit, so uterine blood was the moon-flower supposed to contain the soul of future generations."[2]

In India, menstrual blood is known as the Kula flower or Kula nectar, which is believed to be intimately connected with the life of the family. And when a girl menstruates for the first time, she is said to have "borne the Flower."[3]

Judy Grahn, in her essay "From Sacred Blood to the Curse and Beyond," says about menstrual blood and flowers:

> Among cultures more ancient than our recently patriarchal one, menstruation is equated with flowers and with fruit, for instance, apples and pomegranates... Flowers were seen as wombs, or as the menstruation of a tree or plant. As the tree flowers and makes fruit, so does the human womb flower and make fruit...people used particular flowers to display this connection between women flowering and other things flowering. In many contemporary cultures, the flowers that were held sacred as symbols of the womb are still honored, even though their original meaning has been submerged. In Egypt and India, it was the lotus; in Japan and China the many-petaled chrysanthemum; in Greece the female mysteries of Demeter and her daughter Kore were seen in the pomegranate or the poppy; and for the European-based cultures which spread to the Americas, it was the red, red rose.[4]

1: Menarche: First Blood

SACRAMENT
Janet Ruth Heller

Gazing at your newly rounded bosom
And curving hips,
Your mother smiles with pride.

When you bare the red fountain
Flowing secretly, painfully
From the aroused womb,

She embraces you and whispers,
"This is our shared body
And this our blood."

Menarche: first menses. An event so important in women's lives that most of us never forget when it happened, how it felt, who was there. Yet the word is not in the Oxford English Dictionary, and when I first came across "menarche" in print I didn't know how to pronounce it *because I had never heard anyone say it.*

Menarche (men-ar'-key) literally means "moon" and "beginning": beginning moon, first menstruation.[1]

With the onset of menarche, a girl is potentially fertile, although the first ovulation usually takes place somewhat later. The Jivaro Indians of Equador believe that a woman will not have her first child until after the third blossoming of a tree that blossoms every 6 months.[2]

Menarche can be a very dreamy time, a confusing time, a time when girls feel close to their mothers and at the same time grow more independent. What happens at a girl's first menstruation is very important and can affect her for years to come, influencing how she feels about her periods, her sexuality, her womanhood.

RUST

Kathryn Kerr

She leaned her hot head
against the bus window,
watched the sun set rust-red
over fallow fields
orange with orchard grass
wet in the March wind.
She ached to be alone,
to be gone, to be grown,
Her chest had a catch
that kept her breathing.
Her belly hurt.
Underwear bound her,
it seemed, everywhere.

At home she was caught
in the heat of the kitchen.
Mom said, "Charlie Grider
turned over that old tractor.
Laura found him.
Steering wheel crushed his chest.
There was rust on his vest.
His pipe was broken;
a little blood in his mouth.
We've got to go
to the funeral home.
You can stay here,
study if you want."

Alone she undressed.
There was rust in her pants.
Chilled, she remembered
long orange grass blown
waves over green shoots
on drenched hillsides.
Remembered the moustache
of the man who died
with blood in his mouth.

Unfortunately, for most girls in our society, menarche is a negative, confusing, frightening experience, or, at best, a non-event.

— When I started menstruating my mother frightened me—she told me if I didn't stop bleeding she would have to take me to the hospital. The next day she realized I had reached puberty.[3]

— I was 10 when I got my period...my brother smirked and said, "Here comes the Kotex kid," my father said (leeringly), "Now you're a woman," (I wanted to die), and my mother said, "Well, you'll only have it another 40 years."[4]

— No big deal, didn't tell anyone about it till months later when the family doctor asked.

— My mother said, "Well, now you're old enough to have babies, and your brother's old enough to make someone pregnant, so watch out, you two!"

— It was awful! I started in Mexico. My mother, who'd told me nothing, handed me the pamphlet inside the Kotex box. We were both terribly embarrassed.

— I was afraid. I didn't like it. Made me feel vulnerable and I knew that I was growing up, which I didn't like. Felt self-conscious.

— No one prepared me for it. When I started it was scary,...I told my mother and she laughed at me.

— I spotted the blood early in the morning and went through 6 or 7 pads unnecessarily (my mother had purchased these for me a few months earlier with a simple "you'll be needing these soon") in the first few hours, most of which were spent in the bathroom. When I called my mother at work, I choked up while telling her. She asked why I was crying about it, to which I replied, "I don't know."

— I remember getting my period in eighth grade and not knowing what to do. Another girl told me to tell the teacher. She sent me with a pass to another teacher who said she could give me a pad only if I had a nickel to pay for it. I didn't have the money and had to argue with her, tell her I'd bring it after lunch, while the class listened. Then she handed me the pad wrapped in brown paper towels. All the time I was bleeding through my panties.

— I first got my period on my birthday. I went and told my mother and she SLAPPED me! What a surprise! Afterwards, I found out it was a European tradition.

In Judy Grahn's essay, "From Sacred Blood to the Curse and Beyond," she writes:

Despite any goddess or any ancient menstrual rites, despite Demeter, Mawulisa, Kundalini, Frigga, Ukemochi, Kwan Yin, and all Their temples, sciences, and history, I knowing nothing of them, reacted to my first menstruation in a vastly different way than the spirits of these goddesses could possibly sanction. Like billions of other young women in the violently anti-woman cultures of recent centuries, my menarche was a subject of horror to me, signifying weakness, failure, disability, shame, and a terrible fall in status. From being relatively equal with boys, I became overnight inferior to men...[5]

LILY AT TWELVE

Hilary Tham

Going to the bathroom
every five minutes
knew she was dying
slowly, nobly
suffering while
the family went about
its unconcerned
uncaring way.

Grandmother said
"What's the matter with
the girl? Have you got
diarrhea?" Lily replied
gently, "I'm bleeding,
internal hemorrhage."
Grandmother laughed
"Is that all? You've got
your menses. All women
bleed once a month, it's
nothing special."

Lily did not die though
she wished she had.
Grandmother thought this
her funniest story
and told everyone.

TWELFTH SUMMER

Amber Coverdale Sumrall

June
Mother said I needed it:
a training bra.
I saw tigers jumping

through hoops of fire,
heard the cracking of whips.
She said I had to wear it.
My breasts like fledglings
pushed out of the nest too soon.
July
Dan watched from behind the fence
when Jeanie and I swam naked.
We knew he was there.
Later, he asked me to spend the night
in his tent in the backyard.
Dan was the minister's son so Mother
said I could.
We curled up side by side
in our sleeping bag and kissed,
mouths greedy with unfamiliar hunger.
In the middle of the night
we awakened, shivering,
thinking it was the cold.
August
I started to bleed in Mexico
stained my new white shorts.
Mother hadn't told me anything
but Patsy had.
The drugstore clerk didn't speak english.
Mother pointed at a box of Kotex
on the top shelf.
He had to climb a ladder to reach it.
Everyone saw.
She gave me the enclosure:
What To Tell Your Daughter About Menstruation.
September
I flushed my bloody underpants
down the toilet. It overflowed.
My father asked what happened.
I said nothing.
He brought up the stained white cotton
with the plunger and grounded me for a week.
Told mother she'd have to watch me more,
now that I was bleeding like a woman.
Now that I was coming into heat.

from **RED AS BLOOD**
Karen Loeb

The blood tumbled out of me relentlessly every month and I wore the bulky target bandage between my legs and hated it and was proud at the same time. My brother snickered at me when I said I was going to the drugstore, and I told him he didn't know what I was going for, it could be anything, but the cereal box shaped paper bag gave me away when I came home.

Sometimes it hurt so much I doubled over on the street and my breath galloped in and out and I wondered if I'd make it home alive. I knew I had to because I had to walk the dog and no excuse would be good enough if he shit on the living room carpet.

In the mornings I awoke, aching from the fat bandage and the metal clips pressing into me and sometimes I felt a throbbing between my legs, in there where the blood came from, and it terrified me because I didn't know what the pulsating was and I couldn't stop it and I grew flushed and sometimes cried and I never asked my mother about it.

For some girls it was a better experience:

— I was delighted. I could now have a baby—so at least I knew that much. I also felt very grown-up—very woman. I started the day my grandmother died—seemed significant—like she left me with a gift.

— It was exhilarating! I'd been waiting for it for so long.

— I didn't know how to react. My mom was proud of me and she gave me a light spank on my rear end (a Jewish tradition) and told me to go tell my Dad.

One friend told me she started at her grandmother's house. Her grandmother gently and lovingly helped her to get something on to absorb the blood, and when the girl came downstairs a little later, there were three cups of coffee on the kitchen table: one for her grandmother, one for her aunt, and one for her. The girl felt very proud, because grandmother never gave coffee to "the children."

Many girls get their only information on menarche from the literature in "feminine hygiene" products. This material is too technical and abstract, and it presents the information in a contradictory way, saying the girls are to be congratulated but they must take great care to keep any evidence of menstruation hidden.[6]

Sometimes girls get their first information in a health class at school.

from RED AS BLOOD

Karen Loeb

The blood was different from cuts or bloody noses, it was thick and dark and appeared mysteriously from a place in our bodies that hadn't been injured. In health class we learned to make charts to plot out the Next Time it Would Happen: count twenty-eight days from the first day of your period. And pray for rain, I mumbled. It seemed like the planting charts my grandfather made for his farm, to insure that his corn got as high as an elephant's eye. The health teacher, Mrs. Atkins, distributed calendars to each of us, showed us how to keep a record of our periods each month. Then she told us that the moon had something to do with the whole process, the lunar month being twenty-eight days. The moon pulls at our bodies like it does the tides, she announced, touching her silver whistle left over from gym.

For the next three months my period fell on the full moon which caused me to wait for something miraculous to happen. I told Mrs. Atkins, who only shrugged and said we were studying something else now, and not to worry, it wouldn't happen again. It didn't, and for years I wondered how she knew.

THE WHITE PAD

Phyllis Winston

My mother was modern; she believed in books
with pictures of millions of tiny tadpoles
swimming valiantly up the vast vaginal channel
to certain death, all but one who would survive
to meet the fragile egg.

even so, I did not see why the man and woman
had to be in the same bed when the connection occurred.
she assured me the process was entirely natural.
even I, unique as I was, had been made that way.
I scoffed at her until

in math one day I lost concentration.
my sixth grade teacher began to float
at the board; her column of figures toppled.
I lurched from my seat into the hallway,
through wide swinging metal doors,

to cold white hexagonal tiles, gray stalls
standing at attention. My feet slid across
the floor like tankers crossing the Red Sea,
refusing to be hurried in the face of bombs' blasts.
beyond yellow cinder block walls

the nurse held out the white cotton pad,
its gauze flaps dangling, and two strong
steel safety pins, to anchor the tiny craft
against the surge of the oncoming sea.

Our lack of recognition, let alone celebration, of a girl's menarche is shocking. How many of us were cheered and honored in some way: a special meal, a gift, a party, or a formal ritual? Since most of us don't have a set practice to follow for this occasion, we have to work out the appropriate celebration for our daughters and other girls who have come to this point in their lives. (See menarche rituals at the end of this chapter.)

MOONS AND BLOOD

Elaine Mott

In Woolworth's in 1958
I warmed my cold, December hands
I peeked under the skin of hot chocolate
and sipped through the steam.
My mother, the night before,
had taken me to a film
about menstruation:
there was a girl my age
with a pony-tail and bobby socks,
who had just become a woman;
she was having the hem of her dress
pinned to be shortened;
she was waiting for love.
In Woolworth's they were playing
"Smoke Gets in Your Eyes"
and Christmas carols.
Everything wrapped in green and red foil
shined in the aisles.
I wasted so much money
on rows of pictures of myself
in the curtained booths,
I almost didn't have enough
for the electric-blue eyeshadow
flecked with gold
(that swiveled up and down
in its starred rhinestone casing like a dream)
I bought to make me look Egyptian
while I waited for my life to begin.

Menarche in Literature

Accounts of the menarcheal experience are rare in literature. Anne Frank talks about her "sweet secret." When Emma Goldman's mother saw that her daughter was bleeding, she slapped her—a custom in some Jewish families:

> Suddenly I felt a stinging pain in my face. She had struck me. I let out a shriek, fastening on Mother's terrified eyes. "This is necessary for a girl," she said, "when she becomes a woman, as a protection against disgrace." She tried to take me in her arms, but I pushed her back. I was writhing in pain and I was too outraged for her to touch me.[7]

Mary Jane Sherfey, author of *The Nature and Evolution of Female Sexuality* heard from her girlfriend that menstrual blood was the remains of a dead baby and thus pitied the "little bits of baby" that came out of her. With her second period, she carefully wrapped every napkin and placed them in a painted shoe box, which she tied up with Christmas wrapping. Then, she buried "the baby" in a secret spot and held a funeral service.[8]

Ntozake Shange's *Sassafrass, Cypress & Indigo* provides a wonderful description of how an older woman friend treats a girl when she first starts her period.

> She gently took off Indigo's clothes, dropped them in a pail of cold water. She bathed Indigo in a hot tub filled with rose petals: white, red, and yellow floating around a new woman. She made Indigo a garland of flowers, and motioned for her to go into the back yard.
> "There in the garden, among God's other beauties, you should spend these first hours. Eve's curse threw us out the garden. But like I told you, women tend to beauty and children. Now you can do both. Take your blessing and let your blood flow among the roses. Squat like you will when you give birth. Smile like you will when God chooses to give you a woman's pleasure. Go now, like I say. Be not afraid of your nakedness."
>
> Then Sister Mary shut the back door. Indigo sat bleeding among the roses, fragrant and filled with grace.

Indigo later wants to have a menarche party for her dolls. Her mother is not pleased.

> "Indigo, I don't want to hear another word about it, do you understand me. I'm not setting the table with my Sunday china for fifteen dolls who got their period today!"
> "But, Mama, I promised everybody we'd have a party because we were growing up and could be more like women. That's what Sister Mary Louise

said. She said that we should feast and celebrate with our very best dresses and our very favorite foods."

"Sister Mary Louise needs to get herself married 'fore she's lost what little of her mind she's got left. I don't want you going round that simple woman's house. You take my good velvet from 'tween those dolls' legs. Go to the store and buy yourself some Kotex. Then you come back here and pack those creatures up. Put them in the attic. Bring yourself back here and I'm going to tell you the truth of what you should be worrying about now you such a grown woman."[9]

In juvenile literature, menarche and menstruation seem to be mentioned more than when I was a girl. Judy Blume's *Are You There God? It's Me, Margaret* is an example of a generally positive story of girls waiting to get their periods.

Menarche in Other Cultures

Menarcheal customs around the world range from the beautiful to the horrifying. *Kinaaldá*, the Navajo menarche ceremony, which is the most important of all their religious rites, involves an elaborate five-day-and-night celebration. Here the menarcheal girl becomes Changing Woman, the Navajos' most important deity, and assumes a position of great respect in the society.[10] Menarche in India is also a time for rejoicing: presents, new clothing, ceremonial baths, feasting and shouts of joy. The Tiv of Nigeria make elaborate scars on the girl's body which tell the history of her family.[11]

To the Pygmies in central Africa, menstrual blood is a gift, gratefully and joyously received by the entire community. The girl who has reached menarche goes into seclusion in the *elima* house, taking all her young friends with her, where an older woman relative teaches them the arts and crafts of motherhood. This is followed by a celebration lasting a month or two, and friends come from near and far to pay their respects.[12]

The Navajos and Apaches, who have the most elaborate puberty ceremonies of the Southwest American Indians, are known as mother-right cultures, who "count their descent through women."[13] (See drawing of an elaborate mask used during Apache menarche ceremonies.)

The Mescalero Apache Girls' Puberty Ceremony, an annual event celebrating the menarche of girls who started their periods in the past year, is an elaborate four-day public ceremony, followed by another four days of private observation. Male singers, singing sixty-four different songs on each of the four nights of the public ceremony, recount the history of the tribe. There is feasting, present-giving, and splendid dancing. It is the most important ceremony of these people, and they believe that it insures their survival. Between 1873 and

1911, when the U.S. government made it illegal for the Mescalero Apache to hold these ceremonies, the population did in fact decline.[14]

Across the world, when a daughter in a Japanese family begins her periods, family and friends are invited. The guests are not told the reason for the celebration, but a candied apple or pear adorned with leaves is set on the main food tray. From this, the guests understand the meaning of the celebration.[15]

Other more sinister traditions include severe beatings, female circumcision,[16] and confinement in a small dark cage.[17] The custom of isolating or locking up a girl at the time of her menarche has been explained and justified as being a protective measure not only for the girl but for those around her.[18] The girl's supernatural powers are believed to be so great at this time that she may endanger the entire community. The girl herself is allegedly so vulnerable that she must be protected and given special food. In some cultures, she is isolated not only for protection, but in order to meditate, dream, receive visions, and prepare for her role in the group.

Interpretations

Menarche celebrations in 'primitive' cultures have been explained by anthropologists in many different ways: economic, sociological, psychological and spiritual.

However, as Marla Powers points out:

> Misinterpretation arises from considering individual rites in isolation rather than as a part of a dynamic whole. Puberty ceremonies and menstrual taboos of a culture are never isolated conceptually, and any piecemeal interpretation of them is bound to fail.[19]

A further problem arises from the fact that much of the data on menarche rituals and menstrual customs gathered by 19th century male anthropologists was based on information furnished from male informants.[20] Rituals were too often explained from the point of view of these anthropologists rather than the culture in question.[21]

The sociological, or rites of passage, theory is the most generally accepted explanation of women's initiation rituals.[22] Van Gennep, who wrote *Rites De Passage* in 1909, said the purpose of the ritual was to help the person move from one position in society to another.[23]

According to the economic view, the menarche ritual is most important to the girl's family since the ceremony announces that a new potential wife and mother is on the market. The more elaborate the display staged by the family, the higher price the family may receive for their daughter who will now be able to produce children.[24]

From a spiritual or psychological point of view, menarche rites bestow "cosmic status, a defined place in the universe, and a place of importance and dignity."[25]

Lincoln says of the Navajo initiand,

> Having become Changing Woman, it is she who makes the crops come up, she who makes the seasons change, she who ensures the victory of the Holy People over monsters and chaos...the initiand begins as a person on whom no one depends, and through the course of initiation becomes one on whom the welfare of the entire cosmos hinges. Each time a woman is initiated, the world is saved from chaos, for the fundamental power of creativity is renewed in her being.[26]

There is a certain cynicism in Lincoln's picture of the menarche ceremonies of five cultures:

> There is nothing revolutionary in women's initiation...Cosmic claims notwithstanding, the desired result of the ritual is to make a girl ready and willing to assume the traditional place of a woman as defined within a given culture... Sung over, celebrated, assimilated to the goddess, she is now ready to take up her chores. The strategy is that of placing woman on a pedestal, carried to its outermost possibilities: speak of her as a goddess to make of her a drudge.[27]

Changing The Experience of Menarche

There is no doubt that girls (and boys) should be given a more positive picture of menstruation in their school "family life education" classes. This might help to change society's negative attitudes towards menstruation and women in general. Girls should know that some cultures consider the womb and the blood to be sacred. They should be told about cultures that have menarche celebrations, and encouraged to use their own time of bleeding in a special/creative way. This could include meditating, writing, thinking, being alone, being with a special friend, painting, sleeping or doing "nothing." Girls should also be taught about the causes and methods of alleviating menstrual pain. (See chapter 6: Pain & PMS.) They should be given positive examples of menarche stories from other girls, and should know that this time of their first menstrual periods may be reflected in their dreams. (See chapter 3: Dreamtime.)

In one study of college women who were asked what advice they would offer young girls, the women said girls should be taught how it *feels* to menstruate and about how variable periods can be. They also thought girls should be taught about the options available in sanitary products.[28] The women said they would tell girls, "It happens to everyone and...it differs for everyone"; "that menstruation is not dirty, that it's nothing to hide"; that one should not make "a big deal of moving from 'childhood to womanhood' and not overdo it as being exciting or wonderful"; it should be "as much a part of ordinary life as possible." Girls need to know "that it is a wonderful experience...something healthy...but it's hard to reconcile those positive aspects with the rotten old sanitary napkins and cramps."[29]

> I told her that EVERY woman in the world, even women that none of us (she, I, her mother) would ever meet or couldn't talk to IF we met, women who did not speak our language—and ALL of her friends—ALL WOMEN EVERYWHERE—have periods. I had never realized it that simply before—neither had my aunt. We were all a little amazed and Debbie was enormously relieved. We drank hot chocolate, and Debbie asked if I could sleep in her room. It was the first sentence she'd said since coming downstairs.[30]

Menarche rites have traditionally marked the beginning of fertility, honoring the girl's ability to have children, particularly sons, rather than honoring the girl herself. Since we no longer need worry about producing enough children, we can honor a girl *for herself* at menarche. In celebration, we can teach her about menstruation and how it can affect her life. We can show her how to use this time to "go within" and allow her ample time for sleep and daydreaming. A girl needs to dream, and will do it both day and night.

A woman from Canada sent this description of an experience with her daughter:

> My daughter, Amanda, and I visited Iona, after celebrating her thirteenth birthday. We wandered around the cloisters of the nunnery in the gentle April rain and talked about the power of her first menstruation, not yet come. She was at first somewhat embarrassed, but succumbed to the idea of a celebration for her. The magic of the place played on her too, the daffodils such a vibrant yellow against the subtle greys of the stones, the fresh green of the sheep-cropped grass, the nunnery itself, open to the sky, poignant in its enduring vulnerability. I tried to give Amanda some sense of a history outside of herself, but to which she belonged, the long line of women trailing back into mist. She listened, receptive. I suggested she pay attention to her dreams at this time: they are supposed to be special guides for one's direction in life. A stone cup, a womb-like grail placed on a niche in the wall of piled, cemented stones attracted all my attention. The power of the feminine emanated from it. It was in the room which was supposed to be a refectory—but on the other side of the thick stone wall, outside the nunnery, was a very graphic Sheela-Na-Gig: the Celtic Goddess![31]

Rituals For Menarche

by Beth Beurkens

A ritual for menarche names as well as gives form to the rite of passage which the girl is undergoing physiologically, psychologically and spiritually. Her body is changing, she is growing up inside and her spirit is evolving as well. She is making the passage from girl to young woman on all three levels and ritual can work with all aspects of her growth. As such, it *initiates* her into the new life phase of *young woman* and helps prepare her for this new status.

In Anne Cameron's book *Child of Her People,* we get a glimpse of what menarche preparation was like for girls in the Cree Nation. Starting at the age of 8 or 9, girls spent part of each day together with a specially designated Grandmother Elder. The Grandmother taught them the tribe's creation stories of First Woman, First Mother and the origins of Mother Earth. She taught them what it is to become a woman, about the body's changes and the psyche's growth. The girls learned self-defense from her and practiced on boys in their tribe. They learned herbs to ease cramps and to prevent conception. And when they were fully prepared they then spent time alone, fasting in purification lodges. Only after this year or two of preparation were they then introduced to their people as fully adult women. They were now fully capable of self-survival and had discovered who they were as individuals. They were also seen as *becoming* Mother Earth, fertile, able to create and bear fruit.

Several of my friends and colleagues have performed rituals for menarche with their daughters. These have ranged from simple rituals of creating a special meal together and talking about the young woman's feelings and body's changes, to more elaborate rituals of initiation, choosing a new name, and instruction by older women into the new status of womanhood.

Here are two examples of possible rituals. They are meant as guides and stimuli to your own creativity, to point some ways in the right direction. It is important that the young woman herself should have some input as to its stucture and content, or at the very least, that she be informed of all the steps and give her consent to them.

Honoring Ritual

If you want to celebrate a young woman's menarche in a beautiful way that won't embarrass her but yet will support her and acknowledge the importance of this huge life change, the following ritual will be appropriate.

Have the young woman take a special bath or shower or take her to a sauna or hot tub. She can imagine this bath as cleansing her, washing away the things of childhood she no longer wants, and preparing her for entering adulthood. Flowers and fresh herbs can be floated in the water to enhance the special feeling of the day.

Following the bath, the girl can be given new clothing to wear as a symbol of her new status.

Women friends and women relatives prepare a meal with all of the young woman's favorite foods. Or everyone can meet in a restaurant which has a ritual atmosphere to it. Guests recall their own transitions into womanhood and younger guests can share their expectations. The ceremony can be done with humor and seriousness without any moralizing which adolescents naturally resist.

Following the meal, each guest gives the young woman a gift: flowers, a conch shell, carved images of goddesses, pictures of spirals, lunar calendars, jewelry, new clothing, small makeup kits, books, poems, and quilts. Each guest in turn might say why she is giving it to her and express her wishes or hopes for the future.

Simple and direct as this ritual is, it will give the young woman a clear message that even though puberty is full of change and confusion, it's natural and it's good and right to celebrate this time.

Ritual Of Initiation

You may create a more extensive ritual modelled after those in other cultures which work to initiate the girl into womanhood through a series of steps that include ritual activities. Draw from poems, prayers and traditions as well as from spontaneous ideas of your own.

In a ritual of initiation, separation from the opposite sex and from familiar daily rhythms are important. Fathers, brothers, uncles, boyfriends, grandfathers may, at the beginning of the ritual, recall the girl as a child, share anecdotes and stories about her growing up, and wish her well in her ritual with the women. Thus, the girl is supported in this ceremony by the men and women who are important to her. Afterward, men leave or the women take the girl to another setting to continue the ritual.

The burning of sage or incense during a period of silence is followed by a simple invocation or prayer to the Great Spirit, the Earth Mother or the goddess. Ask them to be with you and help during the ritual.

A simple cleansing purification is then done by washing the girl's feet and anointing them with a scented cream or oil.

Guests should include the initiated, that is, women who have experienced menarche and even menopause themselves. The initiated discuss the passage into womanhood and what it means to a girl in terms of sexuality and the girl's future. This part of the ritual might be called Education with Heart, as you open to the mysteries of the feminine and share them.

Explain also the cycles and phases of the moon and how its rhythms relate to those of women, because awareness of the connections between us and nature is empowering and validates our experience.

The young woman may enjoy the 'test' of spending a night alone in a tent or cabin. There, she may have a significant dream or insight about herself and her future. Following the overnight session, the women will gather again to complete the ritual, asking her to share her feelings and dreams during her time alone.

It is good to do a formal blessing on the young woman to acknowledge her change in life status. A special poem can be read, or a chant said to the young woman, a song sung.

Another way of blessing is for each woman to light a candle and say aloud her prayer or wish for the young woman. Red candles would be symbolic for this occasion. The last candle is lit by the young woman who expresses hopes for herself as an adult woman.

Now comes the time for gift giving. Each woman gives the young woman a gift and tells her why the gift is symbolic of entering womanhood. The gifts and their symbolism might be recorded in a special journal. This journal can then be given to the young woman as a reminder of the ritual and all the affirmations she received. Someone should take photographs of the event.

The ritual concludes with a meal of celebration, music, and whatever else feels festive for this special occasion. You can share the meal in female company only, or the male family and friends can prepare or cater a meal.

Agree to a vow of silence about the female ritual, because talking about it trivializes the experience. A vow of silence is a traditional part of women's rituals to keep them sacred and to reserve them for special occasions. Do not dissipate the power of the ritual by sharing its content with the uninitiated.

Whatever ritual you choose will have a lasting effect on the young woman. She will refer to it again and again as a turning point that gave her the love and support that she needed.

A POEM OF WELCOME

Judith W. Steinbergh

It is a full moon and we are by the sea.
The tide is so high it laps the lip of grass.

What's this? you say over a bright stain of blood.
We both know. All the pulls and tugs aligned

and you stepped to the woman-side
shedding your childhood as simply as a robe.

You must be the daughter of the moon, I say,
and hugging, we buy you small silver hoops

earrings that hold, under your yellow hair,
the secret of who you really are.

Well then, by this single act of the moon,
by this inevitable blooming

you enter our tribe. We welcome you,
one of the youngest, with streamers of pride

and offer our history for strength, our berries for gifts
our force of gravity, love of pleasure, our myths.

1. Testing the Waters

2. Merging Flow

3. Receiving Energy

4. Centering

5. Sending Energy

6. The Struggle

7. Emerging

Just prior to my period...paintings, songs, and poetry emanate from my deepest soul. A clarity, an extreme reality, a sensuous super-sensitivity exists just prior to this physical death and rebirth. -from Mary Beth Edelson's "Menstruation Stories"

2: Seclusion and Power

Seclusion: Punishment or Privilege?

It has long been a custom of women throughout the world to seclude themselves during menstruation. In some cases this is done singly; in others, with a group of menstruating women who set themselves apart in order to rest, heal, receive visions and gather ideas. Isolation may be voluntary or part of an established tradition where women have little or no choice. In fact, in some societies, menstruating women were (and still are) considered unclean, even dangerous, and were intentionally separated from the community. Examples of how menstrual blood is believed to contaminate plants, men, food, and tools are recorded in many cultures.

> And every thing that she lieth upon in her separation shall be unclean: every thing also that she sitteth upon shall be unclean....And if any man lie with her at all, and her flowers be upon him, he shall be unclean seven days; and all the bed whereon he lieth shall be unclean. (Bible, Leviticus 15:19-33)

According to this doctrine, she will also be "unclean" for seven days after the end of menstruation, and on the eighth day must offer two turtles or young pigeons to the priest, one for a "sin offering," the other a burnt offering "for the issue of her uncleanness."[1]

Menstruating women in an Australian tribe are not allowed to harvest food; on one of the New Hebrides islands they may not go near young plants; and Pliny described menstrual blood as "depriving seeds of their fecundity...causing fruits to fall from branches."[2]

These accounts must be held up to what we know about women's close association with agriculture in the history of the world. It is women and Goddesses who are worshipped for fertility, producing both children and the fruits of the earth. But if women can create life, they can also destroy it, and therefore, in certain societies where menstruation is considered unclean, and the menstruous women are thought to be evil, women are forbidden any contact with plants while bleeding.

In 1920, Bela Schick, a German, tried to prove that menstrual blood was toxic, while an American, David Macht, conducted experiments in 1924, allegedly showing the existence of *menotoxins* which destroyed plant life. However, it has not been possible to repeat these experiments. In fact, researchers attempting to duplicate them in 1934 found that non-menstruating women give off more of these toxins than menstruating women.[3]

Women are not afraid of menstrual blood. It's men who believe it can be dangerous to themselves, to plants, and other life. Menstrual blood may have been *taboo* in matriarchal cultures, but was not regarded as evil. In fact the word taboo, from the Polynesian *tupua,* means sacred or magical, and was applied specifically to menstrual blood.[4] Where menstrual blood is associated with evil, there will be found a patriarchal culture. Men have stood in fear or in awe of this monthly bleeding—because of its cyclicity and relation to the moon, because women bleed and do not die, because they don't have this experience, and, perhaps most importantly, because of its association with birth and the power to give life and take it away. Because of this fear, men have suppressed, isolated, controlled, and even killed women who were bleeding.

The aboriginal men in the Kimberleys of northwest Australia, however, as reported by Phyllis Kaberry, never expressed disgust for menstruating women. In fact, there was not even a word in the language which implied ritual uncleanliness.[5]

R. Lowie, writing in 1920, said that the seclusion of women in "primitive communities" was enforced by men as "the consequence of the awe inspired by the phenomena of periodicity."[6]

Women not only bled regularly once a month, they bled together. This synchronicity of bleeding is something many women experience.

— When I get a close female friendship, my cycle will change to hers within one to two weeks of knowing her.

— In the (Air Force) dorm we seemed to hit a cycle among the women.

— It seems to take about six months in treatment for my female patients to menstruate in sync with me. Not that simultaneous menstruation is one of our therapeutic goals; it's just one of those curious bonds that often form between women experiencing rhythms of intimacy....I've been astonished that this unity with my patients has occurred so often, because we are not body-mates. We are not daily exposed to one another's odors. We do not bathe in the same facilities. We do, however, exchange powerful emotional signals.[7]

When women bled together, it allegedly heightened their power. Chris Knight, writing about an Australian aboriginal myth, asks,

> Could it be that the cosmic force feared by men in Australia was nothing other than the force of menstrual cyclicity itself? Could it be that what men feared was that women's flows might—in the absence of rules to isolate women from each other—begin to synchronise, to connect up in a collective 'rhythm' or 'dance' over which men would have no control?[8]

One of the most vivid examples of masculine fear is the reign of terror during the 15th, 16th, and 17th centuries, when nine million "witches" were burned.

> It seems likely that the persecution of the witches in the Middle Ages was one enormous menstrual taboo. How strange and pitiful it is that of all the ways it is possible to execute a person, those that were chosen by the witch-persecutors observe the one law: *thou shalt not spill a witch's blood*. The reason? The power was in the blood.[9]

The torture and ostracizing of witch suspects was seclusion taken to its farthest extreme. Other customs, such as a woman having to thoroughly check herself twice daily to see if she is "clean" after menstruation[10], or rubbing herself with stinging nettles during menstruation[11], while not life-threatening, are degrading and painful. The writers of *The Curse* believe that these humiliating rites were handed down by men and that women were relatively powerless.[12]

Barbara Walker, however, has gathered an enormous amount of data in her *Women's Encyclopedia of Myths and Secrets* showing that women have indeed been in positions of power, particularly before Christianity. "Early writings from Egypt," she says, "depict the woman in complete control of herself and her home, with property descending from mother to daughter." The very word *heir*, in fact, is related to the Greek *here,* a female landowner.[13] The changes wrought by the advent of patriarchal systems and Christianity have greatly demeaned women and, therefore, menstruation. "The holy 'blood of life,'" she writes, "used to be feminine and real; now it is masculine and symbolic."[14]

> Because menstrual blood occupied a central position in matriarchal theologies, and was clearly *sacer*—holy-dreadful—patriarchal-ascetic thinkers showed almost hysterical fear of it.[15]

Vicki Noble, in an article on menstruation, writes that-

> ...until recent history, a woman in her bleeding time was considered to be in a heightened state of awareness and wisdom. In ancient and primitive cultures, women went 'underground' for three days and did not act in ordinary ways. They tuned into their innate psychic abilities at this magical time, opening to oracular messages from the spirit realm.[16]

It is also possible that in societies where men may have forced the women into seclusion, the women in turn used this time in a creative, positive way.

Ruby Modesto, a Cahuilla Medicine Woman, says

> ...the women didn't feel that they were being imposed upon when they retired to the menstrual hut. They got to be by themselves for three or four days. It was a ceremonial occasion which enabled a woman to get in touch with her own special power. It was a time to Dream and have visions. Each month the women went to their own vision pit. The men had vision pits too, places to Dream and pray...This was how the people learned.[17]

Another Native American, a Yurok Indian woman, relates how she is trying to keep the ways of her grandmother.

> A menstruating woman should isolate herself, because this is the time during which she is at the height of her powers. Thus the time shouldn't be wasted in mundane tasks and social distractions, nor should one's concentration be broken by concerns with the opposite sex. Rather, all of one's energies should be applied in concentrated meditation on the nature of one's life, "to find out the purpose of your life."[18]

The Power In Menstruation

What is this power that women have available to them when they are menstruating?

Knight's article on the Australian aboriginal myth states that "These mythical women...are in tune with the immense powers vested in one another's physiologies and blood," referring to the power to give birth. "Is it not *these* powers which are thought 'too dangerous' by men, and which men's taboos and initiation-rites are designed simultaneously to suppress in women, to alienate and to usurp?"[19]

Penelope Shuttle and Peter Redgrove, in *The Wise Wound,* say that menstruation provides women with "inner information" and that "perhaps this is the reason for the universal custom of menstrual seclusion: to enable the woman to draw upon this information."[20]

Apparently among the Greeks, as in innumerable other cultures, the women withdrew at these times, ceased all intercourse with men, and meditated...The woman is held to be taboo at this time, and in many cultures there are tales that the moon herself withdraws for the same reason as other women, that is, to have her period.[21]

The Greeks thought that menstruating women had some power over the earth's fertility and that specific rites evolved for that purpose. Women retired to re-birth themselves, and were in tune with the earth's cycles and fertility.[22]

One of the ways that menstruating women were able to increase the productivity of the earth was by fertilizing the soil and seeds with their menstrual blood. Several women have written to tell me that they use their menstrual blood in this way, either by bleeding directly onto the earth or by rinsing out sponges or cloths and using the water mixed with blood to nourish gardens.

Detail of an Aztec painting that shows a ritual performed by a woman. To 'ensure a prolific crop and to prevent the assault of insects,' a woman walked around a planted field. This painting looks to me like the woman is dragging something in her hand around the field, instead of just walking. An old custom in Italy has a menstruating woman walk around an olive grove to stop it from being ruined by caterpillars. The same story is told of grape vines and insects in France. I believe the Aztec woman is dragging a menstrual pad around the field in her hand.[23] (See illustration, page 29)

Another view is that the real power of menstruation is in its regularity, and that this has benefitted the development of humanity in terms of the measuring of time, counting, and mathematics. Lunar markings found on pre-historic bone fragments show how women marked their cycles and thus began to mark time. Women were the "first observers of the basic periodicity of nature, the periodicity upon which all later scientific observations were made."[24]

Without menstruation and the sciences of measurement women developed from watching first the moon and then the stars, there would be no clocks or watches, no astronomers, no mathematicians or physicists, no astronauts, none of the architecture and engineering which have been born from exact measurement and proportion. We could build a nest, like a bird, but not a pyramid, not a square or rectangular or round or any other regular, geometric shape. Geometry was a gift of menstruation.[25]

The word *menstruation* comes from the Latin *mens,* meaning "month," which in turn comes from "moon," which is is the root of these words also: mensuration (measuring), dimension, immensity, metric, diameter, and many others.[26]

Noble has written that "the mysteries of birth-death-and-rebirth belong to the female, just as they belong to the changing Moon who dies monthly and is reborn. The Goddess-symbol *par excellence* is the snake shedding its skin," she says, referring to the monthly shedding of the uterine lining. Thus, "the menstrual cycle represents healing power...a regular exchange of the inner and outer powers." It is a time for "balance...for going within...for relating to others." The "red" power of menstruation "represents the shamanic healing heat that rises up through the body and regenerates every cell."[27]

The following poem describes women in a Siberian labor camp in the 30s.

THE WOMEN OF PERM CAMP - 80
Irene Zabytko

Women huddled together, oblivious
to the wolf-howling winds,
remember to live when one of them
flows woman-blood,
mystical one who drips crystals
between frost-bitten thighs,

Forgotten daughters of Slavic Amazons,
older than Hera, join hands connecting
broken skin upon skin, radiating warmth,
encircle the anointed one because
she shivers strength enough to
permeate beneath their numbed feet

AND AGAIN
Mary Ernestine O'Dell

As starling flexes tinsel muscle in rhythm
proper for its weight,
as the sleeping body knows to breathe,
the dogwood bleeds its tiny berries.

We are timed by metronomes of planets,
menses blooming red in season,
tide pressing and releasing, as starlings
wing the sky to life in undulant migration.

Winter's blue brings stillness
and the folding of wings,
life-pulse at rest,
but knowing to breathe, and when.

Starlings wait at the far edge of winter.

Seclusion in Modern Times

The need to be alone while bleeding is felt by many women, as can be seen from these comments from the questionnaire.

— On the first day I like to be alone, relax in bed, and read.

— I slow down if possible and tend to read and day-dream more. Prefer solitude, nature...make time to be alone.

— I like to curl up in bed and pamper myself.

— I feel very turned inward. I like to do quiet things. I would love to have a hut to go to with other women.

— I try to avoid having to be out in the world too much (not always feasible!). I live in the country and on a river so those rhythms are important. I also like to sit still in my study with a candle, feeling it flow.

— I try to remember that it is my time to "go-within," to be quieter, relax, do less physical activity. Now I've decided that on my period I will do something I really want to do, but put off because of all my "shoulds"—like reading all day.

— I like to sleep alone (without husband) with my cats.

— I go to the nude beach (weather permitting) and sit quietly, bleeding into the sand. This is my offering.

Individually, we can decide whether or not seclusion is valuable, and if so, how to go about it. Some of us are tied to inflexible jobs or have constant responsibility for our children. If we are unable to isolate ourselves *every* month, it may be possible to be secluded some months. Or perhaps we can do it for *part* of a day while we're bleeding. On days when I feel like being alone, I sometimes lock the doors and unplug the phone while my children are at school. This gives me a few hours, at least, to be completely by myself. Not exactly a glorious "retreat," but certainly affordable and accessible.

In Japan, women who work outside the home can take menstruation leave if they want, but only 13% of them take this leave. This law is being challenged by feminists, who say it leads to discrimination against women and makes it difficult to get equal pay for equal work.[28]

I have talked with many women who would like to have a 'menstrual hut' available to them—a quiet place where menstruating women could be soothed with teas, candles, music and books, soft red pillows, and hot baths. Women could come for an hour or two or a day or more. It would be a place to get away from the world outside and into the woman inside.

A woman from New York wrote that

> For the last few months I have been meeting with a group of other women on the full moon—dancing on the beach...We all have our periods within one week of the full moon, and since this meeting is a conscious celebration of our womanhood, our menstrual cycle is one very positive aspect of that womanhood.

Menstruation, to many, is a healing, powerful, and creative influence.

— It is the force of life. It is the gift of being female. It is more than we know or understand in this day and age. I believe it to be held an honor in our past ages—we've only forgotten.

— I get in touch with a deeper aspect of myself. Menstruation is a time to celebrate your womanly feelings and appreciate the subdued feelings of sensitivity.

— I usually bleed at the dark of the moon and that is when I am most inspired to write.

— Menstruation cleanses and purifies both physically and mentally. It promotes increased consciousness; I dive down deep and resurface with a fuller knowledge and acceptance of myself.

— It's a positive grounding—something we need.

— It allows me access to my deepest emotions. I tend to cry during menstruation, open up my most vulnerable self.

— It makes me more open to the creative, which is what it's all about. Makes me feel at one with the natural cycles of life and death, the great wheel. It definitely provides a clearer access to my writing. I think it's a great blessing. Never fail to feel that sense of awe, even after 20 years!

— Menstruation is my connection to the cycles of the universe—earth, air, sky, spirit. It's one of the most important aspects of my being a woman, for it's not just for propagation, but a time of heightened awareness, insight.

— Every time I start, I feel bonded to all the other women who are bleeding with me.

— Makes me feel very myself, very female, part of nature. I feel I'm operating on all channels—intellect, body, spirit, heart.

— It reminds me that life moves in seasons, cycles. I often lose track of calendar time, but almost always know what body time I'm at.

— I'm much more psychic during my period so I find that an exciting aspect. My blood also seems so alive to me and gives me a certain feeling of power.

THE GODDESS AND ST. VALENTINE

Patricia Handrich

I dreamed of an old friend last night.
She wore a mask, and red,
and she was dancing with the moon.
This morning she phoned to say
she's in town with a troupe of players.
The night comes back upon me—
the power of a vision
only women know.

I dreamed the moon was full
and pulsing.
The moon has her anger too,
changing
always on time.

I dreamed of fire, red masks, red
pistachios, and woke
with a fever.
It is Valentine's Day and I am alone.

My body is puffed and sore.
I bleed and ache and I am happy.
I lie curled in bed
waiting out the pain.
I cannot eat. I break out in sweat.
There are drugs I can take for this
but I don't.
I want to feel this swollen day
and contemplate
the power of the moon and woman.

We worship the rash god Eros
today, and every time we lie together
moving through the ancient dance.
We watch the moon and our moods
in strange anticipation.

I am told I should despise this bleeding
but I don't.
I think of the Sun Dance people
who danced through pain
and sacrificed their blood for love,
the worship of their god.

We learn this every month—
the involuntary sacrifice.
We bend before our goddess,
her cold light and changing faces.
We cry in pain and secretly
we celebrate
our infinite power,
the warm color red.

"Mom! I just had a very strange dream..."
Becky Taylor, Sept. 9, 1983, 2 a.m.

3: Dreamtime

Increased Dream Life

To be aware of our dreams is to know ourselves. Dreams are an important part of the "turning inward" process that women often experience before and during their bleeding. We can use our menstrual time, when our dreams are often vivid and exciting, and when we are more sensitive, open, and insightful, to go deep within. The time of bleeding is a gift, a purely female gift that can enrich our lives.

According to Ernest Hartmann in *The Biology of Dreaming,* we actually do dream more around days twenty-five to thirty of our cycle.[1] These dreams which occur before and during menstruation are often more sexual and striking than dreams we have at other times of the month. Our energy seems to be more, as researchers are fond of saying, "masculine." I prefer to think of it as more "active," rather than "passive," as ovulation dreams are often classified. Certainly, if we are not passive we are not therefore "masculine!"

One study found that menstruating women were apt to dream of speaking animals, animals with men's heads, sex, violence, and broken egg shells, while ovulating women dreamt of jewels, fragile things, babies, conflicts with their mothers, and eggs.[2]

In some cultures it is believed that when we menstruate, we go inward in sleep to meet our "dream husband," or the moon, and have sex with him. A recent study found that it is not uncommon for menstruating women to dream of 'strange men' together with emotions of love, sexual arousal, fear, aversion and fascination.[3] Perhaps we dream of sex because in our waking life we do not always find acceptance for our sexual feelings. Maybe a partner won't make love with us when we are bleeding; or we ourselves are uncomfortable about sex during menstruation. Whether we are conscious of it or not, our sexual dreams may be a guide to what our body desires. In any event, a more intense sexuality is associated with menstruation. (See chapter 4: Menstruation & Sex.)

I CAN'T—AUNT MADGE IS HERE FROM BATON ROUGE

Elizabeth Kerlikowske

Her dream-husband, the moon
drills beams through their open window
five successive nights each month
when he courts the bleeding woman.
Oh but the moon illuminates her pretty face
and on this first night poses his only question
while sipping from a jam jar with
wine is what it looks like:
"What do the red rooftiles mean
sliding off that cottage near Oaxaca?"
The second night when she intends to dream her answer
to this peculiar architectural question,
he bursts through the flimsy curtain.
She's barely asleep
unprepared for this discourse
but they fuck anyway.
It doesn't matter to him.
He just loves the consistency of the red swim,
upstream, salmon.
The moon stays out
flirting with her during the third day
in the backyard where she hangs out the wash.
Sliding into bed, back to her husband's back,
she is greedily receptive to the moon's advance.
They glide in his canoe
and portage across biology
to where the tubes of color are stored.
Like birthdaying children
they squirt them against the walls
reds shot from lipstick zipguns
She loves him in part
because he is not disgusted.
This moon entices her to the sky
the fourth night. She would rather sleep
dreaming of a red ribbon blown across snow
but he agrees to let her be the witch
riding broken eggshells between his face and ours.
She can almost stand it
letting him believe he is the ace flying her there

in this dark place half-crowned with eggs.
To thwart spite
she wakes up.
By the fifth night, though, she is hungry for flesh
and returns to her husband
moved aside for the lover of red
who makes a Magdalen of every Madonna
then turns away his silvery head
until her menses conjure him up again.

Premenstrually, women often have an increase in transition dreams, for example, career changes. Also common at this time are dreams of "inner people" who help and comfort us. One study reported aggressive-type premenstrual dreams "involving difficult journeys with much luggage, shooting, scratching a man's hand so that blood comes, sex with the analyst, dirty water that nevertheless cleans a pail."[4]

BLOOD DREAM
Claudia Frei

We were climbing over rooftops, a tricky, ticklish manoeuvring over the roofs of pleasant cottages on a sunlit day. We slipped in through the top window of a house, very high above the ground, about four stories up.

Below the window, on the lawn, stood a circle of young women with flowers in their hair and wearing light spring dresses. They were tossing a man on a blanket, Eskimo-style, higher and higher, as high as our window. Their intent, utterly unmalicious, was to destroy him. At about the fifth toss the man fell down, down—I felt it in my gut—but the women didn't catch him. His body crushed against the earth.

It wasn't the fall that killed him, though; one of the women smilingly withdrew from him the long dagger upon which he'd been impaled. They'd hidden it under the blanket.

Dreams and PMS

It may be that these vivid, active, aggressive dreams can play an important part in reducing premenstrual and menstrual distress. Hartmann found that premenstrual symptoms are worse when women can't sleep enough and improve when they are allowed to sleep more than usual.[5] Perhaps, says Hartmann, "treatment for premenstrual tension should include a prescription for more sleep."[6] It seems we may have a real *need* to dream before our periods. A disquieting fact is that tranquilizers and sleeping pills, which many women take to ease "menstrual tension," are known to inhibit dreaming.

Shuttle and Redgrove believe that women's undesirable premenstrual symptoms can be dreamt away, as were Penelope Shuttle's. They ask,

> Why do women not enter this dream-state naturally, dream these dreams, and by thorough dreaming avoid entirely the premenstrual symptoms? Is it not likely that the dreaming has been made frightening, just as the menstrual taboo has made the period itself frightening? Is is perhaps that women have particular dreams at this time that are special to women, and the study of which is therefore neglected?[7]

Shuttle and Redgrove maintain that analyzing menstrual dreams in Freudian or Jungian terms is not appropriate, and that "a competent language for the feminine psyche to speak of its menstruation" has not been offered.[8]

A combination of yoga and dreaming has been used to ease and even banish the discomforts of menstruation. Apparently yoga can bring about powerful dreams, and the images in these dreams may then be used in meditation. This gives rise to other dreams, and a sequence develops. "Menstrual distress can be mastered in this way, if the meditations are directed toward the period, and not away from it."[9] (See chapter 6: Pain & PMS.)

Menarche Dreams

Girls sometimes dream of their menarche before it happens. In Michelle Cliff's *Abeng,* a 13-year-old girl dreams of blood falling into a pool on a rock, then wakes in the morning to find she has started bleeding.[10] My daughters both dreamt of their menarche the night before it started. The eldest called me into her room late one night to tell me about a "strange dream." Although she often told me her dreams in the morning, she had never before awakened me in the night.

My daughter dreamed she was at school, and one of the water fountains was overflowing. She tried to fix it, but the rust-colored water kept bubbling over the top. "I guess it was made to do that," she said. When I asked what she thought the dream meant, she said the meaning would be clear later. The next day at school she had "strange feelings" about that water fountain, and that evening, just before dinner, she started her first period.

My youngest daughter dreamed of thick red "sewer water" flowing in the street on the night before her period first started.

Perhaps, if we encourage our daughters to be aware of their dreams, we will find that pre-menarche dreams are not uncommon. And when our daughters begin menstruating, we should know that they may have a real need to sleep more than usual, to dream and day-dream.

Some Native American tribes believe that the dreams a girl has at her first period act as a guide or point to a direction in the girl's life. The menarche rites of the Shasta Indians produce dreams which they believe will come true. The girl is secluded with her mother in a menstrual hut for ten days. At night she is kept awake and only allowed a brief sleep just before dawn. Upon awakening, she tells her dreams to her mother.[11]

Tracking Dreams

Women who keep dream journals might make a note of when they are pre-menstrual and menstruating, and see how these dreams compare with those at other times of the month.

A Canadian, Penny Kemp, sent me her dream journal:

> I am fascinated by dreams that occur pre-period. At this time of heightened sensitivity, my body tells me about itself, different parts portrayed as an orange Volkswagen or a red bull. Often the dreams are powerfully symbolic or prophetic. Either they point out some aspect of reality in my life that I am missing, or they foretell significant details of events that I notice the next day, or six months ahead, as deja vu.
>
> Dream: I am about to serve the family, mom and dad, my husband and my kids, sitting around the table at nanny's. Noticing there's a scum of mold on the red jelly, I scrape what I can off and bring it in. The cherries are embedded in yoghurt from last year, very tangy by now, though the cherries I pick out are alright. (I become aware of the possibility of an infection.)
>
> Dream: The kids and I are at my new flat when my tall, lanky neighbour comes bearing cherry strudel.
>
> Dream: Murray and I are stretched out on limbs of a cherry tree. Coming down, he stuffs as many cherries as he can into his green pantaloons. Third night in a row I've dreamt of cherries.

Brooke Medicine Eagle urges women to "keep a large and lovely book for recording...visions, dreams, imaginings and intuitive flashes." She describes the importance of menstrual dreams in the Native American culture:

> The information received as the menses begins is the clearest human picture from within the womb of the Great Mystery, of the unknown and our future. Among our dreaming peoples, the most prophetic dreams and visions (of the coming of the white peoples and other such almost incomprehensible changes) were *brought to the people through the Moon Lodge.*[12] (italics mine.)

Some women responding to the questionnaire reported that they dream of their periods before starting:

— I often dream about getting my period before I do. I also dream about being fertile when it is my time to ovulate.

— I dreamt last night that I was wearing a pad—knowing I'd be getting my period soon.

— I almost *always* have a 'period dream.' A dream of blood, flow, my period starting, etc. It's like clockwork, very regular.

— Sometimes I dream of blood a day or so before the flow begins.

Women, through the ages, have chosen, or have been forced into, rest and seclusion during menstruation. We would do well to take a lesson from this and take the time, if possible, to relax, to sleep, to dream.

To the question, "Are your dreams different around the time you are menstruating?", women answered:

— They feel prophetic and important. I pay attention to them. They seem more meaningful. I also have insomnia at least one night.

— More visionary—lucid—regressive/receptive. Unravels my soul.

— More people oriented.

— They are more vivid, both in color and feeling.

— Yes. Just before my period I often dream of babies—sometimes of actually giving birth (I never have). Also I often have dreams in which blood is a prominent feature.

— Yes, they usually have to do with sexual fantasies and also with babies.

— Usually more intense and sexual.

— PMS dreams are markedly different—anxiety, paranoia and fear-laden.

— More emotional, lots of people from different parts of my life—lots going on. I throw the bedcovers around more.

— I realized today during my last bloods I had a very impressionable dream with a message I had been seeking.

— I tend to experience deep emotional intensity in my dreams. They are also more vivid and easier to recollect. I feel more connected to the underworld, my subconscious.

MENSES

Nancy Corson Carter

Today my body fills with moon weight;
It shifts dully when I move;
Blood sloughs thickly from my womb walls;
I ache into a monthly primal dream.

Lost among great rocks,
I follow a voice like sand in wind;
(it is the only sound;
my loves are mute and far).

The goddess waits within her cave;
Smiling, she raises her bowl to my lips—
I drink and sign once more:
I am her celebrant and slave.

This tide of hers inside my skin's a
Wild and wedging thing;
Life meets itself, a birthdeath river
Burning moonward.

This dream ebbs, flows with her will;
Entranced, I wait the waking lightness
On familiar shores.

Either the woman is somehow especially desirable at this time, or she is especially desirous, which is to say the same thing.
–Marilyn Nagy [1]

4: The Sexuality of Menstruation

The Tides of Desire

There is little doubt that women feel more sexual around the time of their periods.

— Usually I have more sexual feeling about myself unless I am really having a lot of cramps and not flowing well.

— I usually feel more sexy.

— There are usually a couple of days when I don't feel very sexual, but at the beginning and the end I feel very sexy.

— I feel more in need of making love.

— I enjoy the extra wetness during menstruation. I also like my partner's reaction to my blood. He loves it! Oral sex especially.

— Before, I'm very horny; during, I'm glad not to be touched.

— I love to have intercourse when I'm bleeding a lot and I have turned a few men on to this.[2]

How this sexuality is experienced depends not only upon cultural attitudes, but also upon the extent to which women accept or reject them. As long as we believe menstruation is unclean and unattractive, we will also think our sexuality is unclean and unattractive.[3]

If, on the other hand, we can free ourselves from the negative associations with menstruation, we will find "an enormous power" contained in our menstrual blood, a "sexual element."[4]

In the Tantric tradition, the most powerful sexual rite requires that the woman be menstruating. The blending of the "female red and male white" is very important.[5]

> ...menstrual blood was indeed the wine of poets and sages. It is still specified in the Left Hand Rite of Tantra that the priestess impersonating the Goddess must be menstruating, and after contact with her a man may perform rites that will make him 'a great poet, a Lord of the World'...[6]

It is not "unnatural" to have sex during menstruation. In fact, until the early 1900s, it used to be taken for granted that women would be more sexual while bleeding, because it was assumed that humans, like other animals, bled when they were "in heat," when they could conceive.[7]

Apparently, we simply are more sexual at the time of menstruation. "During the luteal [after ovulation] phase," Mary Jane Sherfey maintains, "the majority of women have a greater spontaneous interest in sexual matters, experience a greater desire to initiate love-making...and achieve multiple orgasms with greater ease."[8] It seems that this increased sense of sexual excitement builds up after ovulation, reaching a peak at menstruation, when the luteal phase ends.

MENSTRUATION
Margie Skelly

That I should love you more now makes sense.
Before I had always questioned this heightened feeling,
but now I know that the answer lies
in the tree meeting the earth
for without the earth, there would be no tree,
no sap to keep the tree alive—
in the horizon meeting the sun
for without the horizon, the sun would shine unseen—
in your body meeting the blood of mine
for without this blood, there would be
no me, no you.

According to Kinsey,

> ...the human female, in the course of evolution, has departed from her mammalian ancestors and developed new characteristics which have relocated the period of maximum sexual arousal near the time of menstruation.[9]

One of the explanations which has been given for woman's sexual arousal at this time is the presence of congestion or edema in the body which builds up during the luteal phase of the cycle. "Women are in a mild state of sexual excitement throughout this period," says Mary Jane Sherfey.[10] The discomfort of this congestion, she says, can be relieved by "frequent and successful" (meaning orgasmic) sexual experiences. In fact, she continues, if the sexual tension goes unrelieved, it can be "a main component of the premenstrual tension syndrome."[11]

I have this idea for inventing a menstrual pad that tickles the clitoris! I'll call them Stim-u-clits...[12]

It is a fact that the clitoris is more sensitive before and during menstruation. Why should we be so sexual at a time when we are not likely to conceive?

— It is as though the mating-signal of genital blood has been wrenched from its former position at ovulation, to a new position at menstruation...as though what this evolutionary step meant was that sex was now to be used for something other than reproduction...[13]

— When I'm bleeding heavily I don't want to be penetrated by a man. I feel a different kind of desire...my thoughts turn to women.[14]

Vicki Noble has described "the infertility of the menstrual period and the dark, passionate sexual power that exists there for its own sake..."[15]

EARLY MORNING LOVE POEM
Katharyn Machan Aal

You touch my womanblood
and with one finger write my name
on the flat curve of your belly,
Blue pillows, talk all night
and now this: love
in the earliest morning hour
when clear eyes seek clear eyes.

We have climbed such a distance
to this bed, to this desire
of mouth for mouth, hands
eager to know private skin
in mutual celebration.

Between us the air turns soft
and disappears.
As mist rises toward the hills
we rise to each other,
gentle, natural,
speaking
in a language
only women make.

As stated in *The Wise Wound:*

> It must be noted that for the woman who is not afraid to have sex during her period, and who has not succumbed to the frequent male taboo on intercourse at this time, her peak-experiences at menstruation are likely to have a completely different tone, and she is likely to have more of them.[16]

Shuttle and Redgrove say this active or "initiating" kind of sexuality is not usually allowed to women, and is therefore often expressed in dreams.[17] (See chapter 3: Dreamtime.)

Too Hot To Handle?

It has been suggested by some writers that menstrual taboos, including seclusion and the avoidance of sex during menstruation, arose out of a need to suppress "women's inordinately high sexual drive and orgasmic capacity."[18] This combination of the female drive and a concurrent male attraction during menstruation was disruptive to the social structure. "...a taboo only arises where desire for the tabooed object is very strong indeed."[19]

C.D. Daly, in fact, believes that the sexual power of menstruation and its blood have been more powerful as an evolutionary force in society than Freud's Oedipus complex.[20]

PMS
Lynn Leone

Pre menstrual syndrome
Makes me like the black widow spider
Any male is eligible
To approach this red dotted derriere
Pleading for performance I later purge my partner
Shedding safety for raw romance
Coupling is not love's consummation

But one partner's sacrifice for my survival
Mating me is tasting poison wine
Passing by the hips, lips but once a month
Staining the bedclothes with blood
Cocooning the corpse beside me
Nourishment for the weaker sex

The bleeding, aggressively sexual female is not exactly held in high regard in our society today. In fact she can be quite frightening to men—but not all men, as the following poem indicates:

REQUEST
Norman German

on black empty nights
the sleeping blood cries
touch me

even at full Moon
the silent blood begs
touch me

Love congeals old and new
into a thick thought
death and Life in one
you and me

blood in war and Love
conjures memory
Love me till you overflow
bright bright Red

Ideally, the men should be able to share in the experience of this rhythm too. If the men do not bend...then they will break, and carry our world down with them. -The Wise Wound, p. 79

5: Menstruation and Men

All of us, female and male, have a memory of our mother's blood—the birth blood, at least, and unless raised by a man since birth, we have intimately known a woman's scents and changes. Most mothers who bottle-feed their babies, and a sizeable number of nursing mothers, too, will be menstruating again before the baby is weaned. And after being weaned, most of us continue to have close physical and emotional contact with our mothers. A friend told me that when he was a small boy he knew when his mother was menstruating by her smell and "softness."

As a child grows and separates from its mother, this connection dims but does not disappear. For a girl, it all comes back at menarche when her body begins to have cycles and rhythms of its own.

And the boys, as they grow into men, and then into older men, react to women's blood in ways that reflect their culture and upbringing.

— I vowed to kiss my daughter's cheek when she reached menarche—but I have no daughter, nor will I have one in the future. But I do have a son, and recently something he said made me realize that I had conveyed to him the healthy, natural, life-giving perspective I had wanted to transmit: I had always been open and casual about menstruation, never hiding it from him when I had my period, and I explained its significance in the birth cycle whenever it was appropriate on a few occasions. When he found out about the blood he seemed to react with distaste at first, but gradually it became a matter-of-fact part of our living in the same home, and I could ask him to bring me a sanitary napkin from the hall closet if I were in the bathroom and needed one. One day when he was nine he gave me a loving pat on my behind as he passed me in the kitchen, and I said he shouldn't do that because I had my period and the pad would be messy (I must have been feeling messy since his spank was outside of my clothing!) "Oh no, Mommy, that's not 'messy'—that just means a baby isn't growing inside you this month!" Well, I smiled, and thought that I had managed to pass on the kiss after all.[1]

In some societies, where it was believed that menstrual blood was sacred and the key to all life, men were thought to become immensely powerful by "absorbing" menstrual blood.

> Taoists said a man could become immortal (or at least long-lived) by absorbing menstrual blood, called red yin juice, from a woman's Mysterious Gateway...Chinese sages called this red juice the essence of Mother Earth, the yin principle that gives life to all things. They claimed the Yellow Emperor became a god by absorbing the yin juice of twelve hundred women.[2]

BLOOD KNOWING
Charles Fishman

Your blood
on the sheets—
a dark red flag
that has pulled free
of your body.
I lay claim to it,
to learn the
boundaries.
This is blood
to swear by:
what is within you
will be tasted.
I will know you
entire, will risk
drowning,
though I go down
spinning
into my own
confusion.

One of Portnoy's complaints, to illustrate men's negative reactions, was the fact that his mother menstruated. He once saw two red drops of her blood on the linoleum. Twenty-five years later, still upset by these two drops, he put them in his "Modern Museum of Gripes and Grievances."[3]

MENSTRUAL BLOOD
Carol Stone Ptak

Menstrual blood
he fears it
as exuding disease;
"unclean" a leper's
vile festering sore
dripping death.

Menstrual blood
she reveres it
as crimson renewal;
a pulsing flowing
timeless tide. Venerable
wine of life.

A different point of view was sent in by a woman on the questionnaire:

— It's easy to talk about menstruation with my boyfriend and always has been. They all seem to have a healthy, positive attitude about it, and have had no qualms about sex or even oral sex at those times, and are considerate of pain and moodiness. I think that many men are moving in that direction, rather than the "she's a hag on the rag" attitude.

Men's Envy of Women

Women's rhythms, their connection to the moon's cycle, and their ability to give birth have all been a source of envy to men, as seen in myths throughout the world and the many references to "magic blood." An old Australian story tells of men who are openly jealous of women's blood, and steal it to use for their own magic. The men confess that they "have nothing to do really, except copulate, it all belongs to the women..."[4]

It has been suggested that men may have taken over the wand or baton, the instrument used by women originally to mark menstrual cycles, "because it was a most ancient symbol of feminine power. The priest and the shaman dress like women to take on their magic..."[5]

Bruno Bettelheim has written that men's blood-letting rites, such as circumcision at puberty and the American Indian Sundance come from a desire to obtain the "magic blood."[6]

Another rite, called subincision, involves slitting the underside of the penis so it resembles a vagina.

The idea is that when the split penis is held upright against the man's abdomen it resembles a menstruating vagina. This extreme operation, or subcision, is done in New Guinea, Australia, the Philippines, and Africa. In some places in New Guinea, the word for the cut penis is the same as a word meaning "the one with the vulva"; in others the blood that is periodically caused to flow from the wound is called "man's menstruation." Another people say that the blood flowing from the wound is no longer the man's blood: Since it has been sung over and made strong, it is the same as the menstrual blood of "the old Wawilak women."[7]

"It is hard to imagine a more dramatic example of woman envy," says Paula Weideger, referring to subincision. "Obviously menstruation is not universally believed to be a curse, although it may be that menstruation is universally envied."[8]

All of these male blood rites, including the slash in Christ's side (at uterus-level, says Phyllis Chesler) and his bloody crown of briars, the bloody bandages on the war heroes, have been interpreted as men's attempts to imitate 'menstrual' magic. They all, says Judy Grahn, "have a similar underlying formula: The ability to shed blood equals the control of life powers."[9]

Phyllis Chesler, in her book *About Men,* writes:

Thinking about men, I began to realize the significance that blood has for men as a symbol of violence and death, and not as a symbol of a normal biological event. Consequently, men are irrationally afraid of blood and are especially confused by female blood. Female blood is feared, isolated, punished and, strangely, envied by men.[10]

The connection has even been made between a society's attitudes toward menstrual blood, and the aggressiveness of that society. "...if there is no acknowledgement of the women's natural shedding of blood, then blood still has to be shed somehow, in warfare if necessary." Ruth Benedict said for the Amerindian Kwakiutl, a very war-like society, menstrual blood was thought to be extremely polluting.[11]

Men's Fear and Control of Women

Several theorists suggest that it was men's fear of women that gave rise to menstrual taboos and control over women.

Men fear the synchronicity of women's bleeding, according to Chris Knight, as well as their reproductive power and the "solidarity of the feminine sex." The men's imitation rituals, therefore, were for the purpose of taking away women's power and transferring it "to the community of men."[12]

Durkheim believed that men's fear of women and menstrual blood was so strong and so vital to the clan that it provided solidarity and structure to the society.[13]

Men's fear of menstruating woman's power is reflected in many taboos. Bleeding women have been kept from handling religious paraphernalia at the altar; they have been hidden behind the walls and curtains in the synagogue; and excluded from certain American Indian rituals.

> Male blood-letting is considered "cleansing," while at the same time natural female blood is considered "dirty." The concept of ritual uncleanliness was used by men to suppress woman's sphere of influence...to demean matriarchal customs.[14]

MISNOMERS

Natalie Safir

How did they manage
to get it all turned around

so that we were second
or less, translating
"rib" instead of
"side", the two parts
integral?

Firmament/stars
continents/oceans,
without one, there
is no other.

How did they learn to forget
Earth was the mother,
the amniotic Sea the source,
misnaming Eden and
citing the MacIntosh
instead of the tough-skinned
pomegranate
woman would know was hard
to bite, slightly bitter
and complex at center?

How did they get it wrong
about the power of water,
the pull of tides,
the origin of insight.
Were there in fact, only
three wise men?

Judy Grahn talks about what patriarchy has done to menstruation:

> From its splendid history as a great public socializing force...from a position central to human culture and the door through which females entered into the full status of adulthood with political and scientific clout — menstruation has been violently reversed over the centuries into a private, shameful act, equated with being slightly ill or weak...The status and social control women have had has fallen with the fall of menstruation.[15]

The control of women through menstruation is seen today in the treatment of pre-menstrual syndrome. PMS is being "managed" in a way that is not in women's interests. Women's real concerns are ignored; PMS is labelled an illness and a cause of anger and frustration. (See chapter 6: Pain & PMS.)

Women's bodies are ever-changing, in a way that men's are not. Men can not really know what it is to be a woman, but if they greet the rhythms of a woman's body with openness and wonder they will find their own lives enriched by contact with depths they can never directly experience.

MENSES
Robert Gibb

1
At night you rise
On all fours
On the bed and look,
Wondering is it now,
Has it started,
Wondering
Whose body this is
Which is capable
Of such sacraments.

2
None of the mysteries
Is deeper than this
Blood at the heart
Of your own calendar,
The round sequences
Which slide in
And out of the body
Like the perfect
Phasing of the moon.

3

It is the red flower
That blooms by the roadbed,
The dark red bird
Whose song is blood,
The miracle of you,
This dark which keeps
On bleeding, these petals
Which are always healing
Within themselves.

MEN! YOU'RE ALL ALIKE!

GEEZ! WHAT'S BUGGING AVA?
I THINK IT'S THAT TIME OF MONTH.
YOU MEAN SHE ACTS THAT WAY BECAUSE THE RENT IS DUE?
NO, NO...

...IT'S BECAUSE...
UH, ACTUALLY I DON'T REALLY KNOW WHY. IT'S A MYSTERY.
WELL, THAT'S DUMB!
I'LL JUST GO ASK HER.
OKAY, KID.. BUT KEEP YOUR GUARD UP

Later...
HI, KID... WHAT'D YOU FIND OUT?
MEN! YOU'RE ALL ALIKE!
I TOLD YOU TO KEEP YOUR GUARD UP.
TIM EAGAN

Suppose that society is a lie, and the period is a moment of truth which will not sustain lies. - The Wise Wound, p. 58

6: Pain and PMS

Even though this book has as its theme the celebration of menstruation, it would be incomplete without a discussion of the pain, both physical and emotional, that a great many women experience before and during their bleeding.

Nearly half of the poems I received in response to my calls for material for this book were about the pain and depression that often accompany menstruation, including several accounts of embarrassing or frightening menarches. Since I wanted a more positive response, I put the ad in a leading women's magazine leaving out the word "pain." The ad read: "Menstruation celebration—stories, poems, art work sought for anthology on the celebration and positive aspects of menarche, menstruation, and menopause." The response was relatively small.

Many of the poems I received which were in fact celebratory also alluded to a certain amount of pain. For some women pain is an integral, accepted, expected part of menstruation, even when their feelings are generally positive, as is shown in the following two poems.

THE MAINSTREAM
Barbara Crooker

...all one's actual apprehension of what it is like to be a woman, the irreconcilable difference of it—that sense of living one's deepest life underwater, that dark involvement with blood & birth & death...[is lost in our society.] Joan Didion, *The White Album*

That time of month.
All day long I am under
water in anticipation.
My stomach slogs and sloshes

like milk in a jug carted
over a rocky road.
The sullen moon pulls out
the balance;
the monthly tide returns.

Swaddled in water, cradled in salt,
we lived nine months in the current
before that first swim,
the gush and run
of the birthing flood,
when the water broke
on boulders and we fell
into the alien air.
Not fish out of water,
we survived, grew older,
watched the grass swish and eddy.

But once each month,
our quivering gills remember.
We swim again in the mainstream,
touching the current.
We know what is real:
birthwater, bathwater, milk & manna.
My woman's hair
rivers out behind
like tributaries
seeking the sea.

MY VALENTINE

Janice Eidus

I'm bleeding
Red and scented like a valentine.
Or a warm glass of burgundy wine on a tablecloth
Checked red and white.

Inside me is the sunset colored wildflower
Bleeding its colors on the field
Juice stemmed, sugar petaled.

Most months I've cried raw.
Yet today I laugh with a mouth red, with
Scarlet drops of honey on my lips.

Inside I am as vivid as the planet Mars
On fire
Orbiting within the waters of the Red Sea,
And emerging pure, pure and
Bleeding this special red,
This honeyed red,
This scarlet, my scarlet, my love.

From Acne to Agony

What exactly is the pain and discomfort of menstruation? Most writers on menstrual pain separate it into two categories: first, PMS or PMT (pre-menstrual syndrome or pre-menstrual tension) which is usually described as irritability, depression, achiness and bloating; and second, the cramping and physical pain, called dysmenorrhea, which generally occurs while bleeding. My own experience with various menstrual discomforts is that they do not fit neatly into the-kind-you-have-before and the-kind-you-have-during.

IF WELL BUILT FOR SUSTAINED ASSAULT

Bonnie Gordon

The moon is full tonight and everything must live. When you talk to me today, I feel acted upon. Nothing in this town subverts anything else. I told someone I loved to go away. I accused someone else of failing to adore me enough. There are voices in the darkness I am straining to hear. I spoke to no friends today. I bled much. I burned few calories. I felt intimidated in a bakery. All day I am reminded of powerlessness. All day I kick tires, spit at iron, tear at ropes. The sun granted an audience for only a brief period. I failed to show up on time. I was unable to perform even the most minor transactions in the cool world. I jumped when someone touched my skin. Gravity is pulling me down. The moon pushes at me, smirks, then picks me up, dusts me off, and lifts my gaze with a single finger, until my lowered resisting gaze is forced to meet hers straight on. Everything hurts me. My back hurts me. My son's scrapes hurt me. I can't breathe very well. I feel too heavy on the ground. My chest is tight. Something inside me is wounded. I want the jungle below the concrete to emerge, I want these houses drowned in jungle brush. I slip in and out of my skin like a silk glove. I wish I were anywhere but here. I touch my face, my hands, my legs, approve a perfect fit. I sense a cord, let it snap. A glance in the mirror shows a watercolor shadow. Gravitational anarchy, a rocking motion. You just don't seem to be here tonight, he said. Looking back, I don't like much of what I remember, though I long for it all the same.

Primary dysmenorrhea is better known as "cramps" and is not caused by any physical abnormality. Secondary dysmenorrhea, however, is caused by particular problems such as fibroid tumors, pelvic inflammatory disease, or endometriosis.

The syndrome of pre-menstrual discomfort was first described in 1931.[1] The symptoms appear at some point after ovulation and disappear at the beginning of the menstrual period. These symptoms are different from dysmenorrhea, which is better understood than PMS.

It is said that 90% of menstruating women experience some degree of premenstrual tension. The symptoms described, however, include breast tenderness, water retention, increased appetite or thirst, and constipation.[2] While these premenstrual feelings may be uncomfortable, they do not constitute "illness."

An article in *Psychology Today* states that 70% of menstruating women "notice at least one change in the week or so before menstruation." Actually, 100% of menstruating women could be expected to notice *some* change. We would have to be very unaware of our bodies not to experience its changes. About 12% of menstruating women are said to experience *positive* changes, "including increased energy, sensitivity and creativity, heightened arousal and desire for sex and a general feeling of well-being." According to this article, the negative changes are usually mild to moderate, accepted by most women as a natural part of their monthly cycle.[3]

It should be pointed out that most of the questionnaires which are used by social scientists to determine what women feel during menstruation offer only negative choices. An example is the Menstrual Symptom Questionnaire, developed in 1975. If a woman did feel positively about any part of her period, there would be no place to put it on this questionnaire. No one, in fact, has systematically described or studied the positive effects of menstruation.[4]

Menstrual distress, however, is definitely a part of life for many, many women. When Judy Lever did a TV documentary in England on PMS, though scorned by her male colleagues, it generated the largest number of responses ever received from a documentary. The letters and calls were heartbreaking, she said, full of rage, depression, and "a terrible sense of isolation."[5]

Her book, *Premenstrual Tension,* was written in response to the women's cries of despair.

EACH MONTH

Arleen Cohen

a prisoner
of the moon
whose lunar hand
pulls the seas.
high tides
carry me out

low tides in.
sometimes sucked
into a vortex
of cold, dark water.
from the bottom
I struggle
to the top
and stroke
for the shore.

UNTITLED
Rhonda Collins

a warm surge
like a newborn thing
painful greetings
again

welcome relief
back at last from that
seemingly perpetual melancholic place
where no single thing exists
to fill that cavernous hole
no single imaginable thing
to make life seem purposeful?

but a quiet thought
of a red circular painting
with a blackened area, a hole, and
crawling through it
to some other place.

Why This Discomfort?

A handout from the Santa Cruz Women's Health Center states that possible causes of dysmenorrhea or "cramps" are: mineral imbalance, too much progesterone in the body, an extreme sensitivity to progesterone, or an overproduction of prostaglandins."

The causes of pre-menstrual syndrome have also been attributed to hormonal and chemical imbalances in the body. Katharina Dalton theorizes that if the ovaries do not produce enough progesterone in the last half of the cycle, progesterone may then be taken from the adrenal glands, disturbing their production of corticosteriods. This imbalance of corticosteroids results in further imbalances in the body of sodium, potassium, blood sugar, and lowered resistance to infection, which could account for various premenstrual symptoms.[6] However, a 1976 study found that depression, a major symptom of PMS, is unrelated to hormone levels.[7] And Adelle Davis says depression could result from the fact that a woman's level of calcium falls considerably during the week prior to menstruation.[8]

Lever suggests that the cause of menstrual distress is primarily physical, but she cites cases where a change of attitude reduced the symptoms. If women respected their bleeding, were not ashamed of it, did not feel they needed to hide it, might this not ease their PMS? She says PMS sufferers are often women whose parents were embarrassed to talk about the subject, thus creating negative attitudes.[9]

A vicious circle surrounds the cycle: the negative attitudes to menstruation found throughout this society cause women to feel bad about themselves while menstruating.[10] This in turn affects the way the women act, and the resulting "unacceptable" behavior (often described as being "bitchy" or "on the rag") reinforces the negative attitudes. We are so conditioned to feel poorly before our periods, that women have been found to say they have PMS if they *think* they are premenstrual, even when they're not.[11]

One study found that PMS often coincided with stress in the family or work situation.[12] And the examples given, such as being fired, or suddenly becoming a divorced working mother, are cultural conditions which would probably not be alleviated by a change in attitude.

Pain and irritability can also be caused by frustrated sexual feelings, particularly if the woman is sexually aroused at menstruation and her partner is turned off. There may also be physical discomfort due to the premenstrual build-up of fluids in the genitals, which is relieved with orgasms.

Another view is that 'arousability' is what changes during the menstrual cycle. Both negative *and* positive emotions are increased during the premenstrual phase, but the culture defines negative feelings as "premenstrual." Positive feelings are in most cases attributed to other causes, such as a sunny day.[13] The way we perceive these feelings determines what we call them.

Gynecologists have told women that their menstrual disorders are the result of their resistance to the role of wife and mother.[14] These doctors say women should change their attitudes about their life situation and accept society's definition of what women should be. This is not at all the same as becoming more positive towards menstruation and accepting oneself as a woman in control of her life. This more constructive attitude, in fact, is at odds with traditional roles. A liberated woman is more likely to throw off the negativity surrounding menstruation, which in turn may ease menstrual disorders.

Paula Weideger found that in her women's groups, "it soon became obvious that most of the problems with menstruation and menopause result from physical malfunction or cultural pressures," and were not psychological, as the "gynecologist/shaman" would have us believe.[15]

A woman gynecologist in Massachusetts believes that a good deal of PMS is iatrogenic—caused by medical treatment. Women often experience it for the first time after going off the pill, after tubal ligation, or after a hysterectomy if the ovaries have been removed.[16] One researcher found that most of women's menstrual problems were related to "traumatic or badly handled experiences of the first period."[17] Another suggests that perhaps PMS is the collection of all the bad feelings of the month felt intensely during the premenstrual period.[18]

These studies indicate a wide variety of theories about the causes of PMS. Surveys are biased to some extent by the researchers' assumptions. Women who are troubled with PMS may have to search for the causes themselves. The medical profession, though helpful in some cases, cannot be relied upon as the only source of answers to questions about women's bodies, because it has a history of anti-woman prejudice.[19]

For Help with Menstrual Discomfort

Some women, like Judy Grahn, have found a change of diet enormously helpful. Others swear by herbs, exercise, and orgasms for alleviating both PMS and cramps. Still others say nothing at all helps. One woman I know had severe cramps for years. To her immense surprise, after talking about her periods *for the first time* (in a women's studies class), she had no cramps during her next period.

Home remedies that work for some women include: heating pad, lying in the sun, massage, orgasms, jumping into cold water, regular exercise, yoga (especially The Plough), deep breathing, increased intake of calcium and magnesium before and during menstruation, over-the-counter preparations, alcohol (a relaxant which also stimulates blood flow), fasting one or two days before menstruation, and herbs. (See Parvati in Resources and Readings, Appendix II.)

Many women believe that diet is the key to easier periods and nothing can overcome the effects of a poor diet. The first step is to limit refined sugars, fats, chemical additives, processed foods, alcohol, beef, caffeine, grapefruit, oranges, chocolate, dairy products, and potatoes.[20]

Judy Grahn says:

> I eat quite differently—and I love my period. Sometimes I need one aspirin for it. Mostly I take nothing except long soaking baths.

Grahn's severe cramping was eliminated with vitamin E, whole grain breads, brewer's yeast, "and cereals that still have their living cells intact and full of B vitamins."[21]

The Boston Women's Health Book Collective urges women to "Make sure the food you eat is varied, sufficient and balanced.... Pay attention to the positive and negative effects of what you eat. Many women find it helps to eat *more* whole grains, flours and brewer's yeast and *less* salt, sugar and caffeine."[22]

— Too much coffee makes my usual premenstrual breast tenderness quite intense (increase in fibrocystic tissue) but I don't interpret this feeling as pain.

— I used to have severe cramps on the first day. I tried many things over the years: my mother would put me to bed and give me warm wine; I tried Midol, codeine, Vitamin B_6 and calcium (works well!), whiskey, Tiger Balm on my lower back (very relaxing), heating pad in bed, Valium. It seemed that the best thing was to sleep for a few hours, and the muscles had a chance to relax, and upon awakening I wouldn't have any pain. About seven years ago, though, since there wasn't a method that worked every time, I decided that it was psychological—it was a good attention-getter—and decided to use mind over matter, that I no longer needed the hassle. This has worked the best. It's not a problem any more and I also use B_6 and calcium.[23]

The BWHBC also suggests that women increase their potassium (bananas, fresh orange juice, peanuts or peanut butter) and reduce liquids. They warn that if diuretics are taken, this can deplete potassium. For tiredness: sleep, of course—more than usual may be needed. Iron-rich foods are also recommended: blackstrap molasses, beans, raisins. (Liver has a lot of iron, but it also stores the chemicals fed to animals.) For very heavy flow they recommend increased intake of calcium.

One doctor found that most of her patients responded to a hypoglycemia diet: whole grains, no caffeine, lots of water, no sugar, frequent small meals, and vitamin B_6. Another doctor reports that about 80% of all cases of PMS are helped by reducing salt intake and taking vitamin B_6.[24] However, too much vitamin B_6 may be toxic. "Dosages of 500 milligrams per day or more can cause a variety of neurological disorders, including numbness in the feet, hips, hands and face."[25]

Yet another source maintains that taking a placebo does as much good as taking vitamin B_6.[26]

The administration of progesterone is another controversial treatment for PMS. It is widely used by Dr. Katharina Dalton in England, who says women "owe it to themselves" to get treatment; if they don't, they "will get what they deserve from men."[27] While Dalton is quite sincere, it is worthwhile to consider whether or not men instantly seek medical answers when they are irritable or feel violent. Furthermore, although progesterone treatment is used by thousands of women, there is no direct evidence that PMS sufferers have lower levels of progesterone than other women.[28]

Dalton defines PMS as any symptom that recurs premenstrually. She believes these symptoms should be automatically treated with progesterone, which is not the same as treating symptoms if and when they occur. The fact that symptoms occur in a cycle does not prove that the cycle itself is the problem.[29]

There has not been one convincing study in either the U.S. or England on the efficacy of progesterone on PMS. Users often take more progesterone than their doctors prescribe. Some of these women bleed all the time and others don't menstruate at all. Swelling of the vagina and rectum is common, and breast tumors, cervical cancer, and chest pains have also been reported in women taking progesterone.[30]

Progesterone therapy is a nonspecific and very expensive approach to treating PMS. Many physicians will not prescribe this drug at all because the effect of high doses in the long run is not known.[31]

In two studies which have compared progesterone with a placebo, it was found that progesterone worked no better than the placebo.[32] Researchers also claim that fifty percent of PMS sufferers respond positively to placebo treatment. Perhaps women are so relieved when their complaints are taken seriously that the placebo has a positive effect.[33] For the physical pain of dysmenorrhea, however, placebos and psychological suggestion are apparently not effective.[34]

It is important to accept the reality of PMS feelings, but it is not healthy to conclude that they are abnormal and must be eliminated. Detachment from bodily rhythms can lead to illness, and this in turn leads to further 'distancing' of a woman from her body.

Some women take tranquilizers to "get them through" their pre-menstrual days. Tranquilizers, however, cut women off from their feelings, their dreams, their sex—all of which are intensified premenstrually and could actually enhance their lives. Women should ask themselves what is going on in their lives that they need to tranquilize, and who benefits by their being tranquilized.

MENSTRUAL MEDICATION

Ginger Porter

One yellow pill
quiets
the maddening bouquets
that bloom in my mind,
screaming at me
in bright colors
of mis-matched emotions.

Blatant colors
fade to pastels
behind a valium sheen.
Another pill
melts the cold, metal
knives of pain
that slash through my
innocuous womb.
The passive white tablets
are ground
back into opium powder
by the churning knots
in my stomach.
Pulsing, throbbing
velvet vessels
transport the potency
that turns my muscles
to Jell-O,
blotting out my inner vision,
blinding my brain cells
until I wake
to the gush of blood
and the shock of scarlet.

Acupuncture treatments for PMS have been very successful in some cases. One woman I interviewed had very severe PMS ever since she started her periods at age 10, and it became even worse after the birth of her child. At ovulation, she became depressed, suicidal, had eating binges, bloating, and extreme anxiety. This continued until her period started, at which time it stopped immediately. She tried diet changes, exercise, vitamins, and was told by her doctors that perhaps her illness didn't really exist. She, however, knew it was physiological. She read about progesterone but her doctor wouldn't prescribe it. Then someone suggested she see an acupuncturist, and this resulted in immediate relief. After seeing the acupuncturist, her next period arrived without symptoms. In fact, she was unware that it was due. Since then she has not suffered from depression or any of her other symptoms. At first she saw the acupuncturist three times a week; now she sees him once a week; later it will be once a month. She knows of other women whose PMS has been helped by acupuncture, and her acupuncturist says several women come to him for treatment for PMS.

In summary, each woman's cycle is unique and variable from one month to the next. When we suffer PMS symptoms we should look critically at our life situation (Are we doing what we want? Should some things be changed?), our life-style (diet, exercise, relaxation) and our attitude toward menstruation, factors definitely associated with menstrual distress. Even so, some months will be worse than others, and medication or other treatment may be needed. And some women may need this every month.

The following menstrual journal by Miriam Sagan shows the variability, the pain, the dreams, and the exhilaration in one woman's cycles over a year's time. Sagan says writing this journal was part of a monthly ritual for her. I would urge women to keep such a journal to get a perspective on their moods, their pain, their lives.

February 16, 1979. Saratoga Springs

Pre-menstrual, breasts swollen. Dreamt about time warps. H. transports his bureau home via a time warp. I try to ride in it but meet a giant or perhaps a guardian. Then have a horrible dream about trying to call Devon on the phone. Confusion about her last name—married or maiden? Also, dreamed again that I had lung cancer.

The toilet is overflowing and I am sure it is my fault, as I flushed some tampax down it. Now, I hear workmen flushing and pumping, and I hide in the far corner of my studio reading a biography of Colette written by her third husband; and I am pretending to be a stone or a piece of furniture and not a menstruating woman. Thinking for some reason a great deal about the holocaust. Falling asleep at night, I fantasize that I will learn Hebrew, read about Judaism, go to shul. I am full right now with plans for my life.

March 12. Boston

Morning dream: I live through the holocaust, I am a survivor. In a relocation camp I develop a burning desire to go to Palestine rather than to America. I call my father from a pay phone. He asks me if I need to take an achievement test to get into Israel—I say no, I won't even learn to read and write the language, jusk speak it. He encourages me to go. I get on a long line of people boarding through a chute.

Windy cold day. Menstruating. Real cramps. What moon is it? Menstruated at the full last month. Speaking French to the cat. Good thing Sue is coming by, have been alone for over 24 hours.

April 8. Boston

Menstruating. Palm Sunday. Saw people carrying green fronds on the trolley. Cold. Wind and sun. Afternoon ghost moon in the sky. Began to bleed standing in the Museum of Science, watching a Rube Goldberg-like contraption on kinetic energy. Bled into my khaki pants, as I was wearing no underwear. Odd, I had had a menstrual consciousness for a few days—even planned on writing about it, and my breasts were swollen, but I had totally neglected to pack a tampon. There were none in the "ladies" room, and I didn't even have a dime on me. Finally, stuck a wad of paper up my vagina, but this was uncomfortable. Looked around for a woman to ask for a tampax. Became suddenly aware of everyone's menstrual status: noticed who was post-menopausal, who was pregnant. Finally got up the nerve to ask a nice looking woman with three little girls. She produced a tampax and smiled. "You've saved my life!" I told her. The little girls looked curious. I felt a mixture of relief, embarrassment, and exhilaration. Continued around the museum. Felt a surge of interest in the exhibit on reproduction, the cross section of ovaries. "That's me!" I wanted to say. Then, felt sudden exhaustion on the subway coming home. Bleeding, bleeding. Exhaustion under my eyes, cramps. Yet energy flowing beneath the fatigue. Felt exhilarated, ultra-sensitive.

May 8. Boston

Menstruating: two days late, was already having pregnancy fantasies. Imagined sitting in the waiting room of an abortion clinic. Almost more of a wish than a fear. Every period the loss of a potential child; loss, sadness, even though there is no room in my life for a child now.

Menstruation: the crack between the worlds. A woman sorcerer is at the height of her power when she bleeds. I welcome the blood. I've awaited it this month, prepared for it.

June 6. Santa Fe

Tripped our brains out last night. The beginning was the most frightening. My knees were on fire, molten orange, they were flowing into each other when I pressed them together. I could see auras of fire in my feet. Today, actually felt good, despite my period. I felt frightened tripping pre-menstrually—too large a crack between the worlds. But the blood flow feels good, a return.

July 3. Boston

Red flag: buoy marking shoals, danger, do not swim past this point. Red flag: stop, gas meter on empty, no room at the inn. When you left me last summer, love, you left me a thesaurus. Red: scarlet, vermilion, crimson, maroon, magenta, ruby, damask, cerise, Pompeian red, hellebore, cardinal, Indian, Chinese, carmine, burnt lake. And the comparisons, red as...garnet, bloodstone, rust, lobster, cranberry, and although not mentioned, red as... blood, menstrual blood. I open my legs and out flows a red sea. Warning: I am exquisite; I bleed and do not die. I burn and am not consumed.

Red flag.

August 1. Boston

Feel very low. Depressed, suicidal. Menstruating. Physically shakey, spacey. No energy. No mail. No phone call.

August 27. Boston

Menstruating. Hideous exzema. Last night a red rash grew and spread over my face. My neck covered with scales. I was turning into a lizard, a snake. Scales on my nipples. Red poison patches under my armpits. Inhuman, marked, snake woman. Keeping my head down, afraid of the look of a passer-by.

September 15. Boston

Feel fat, bloated, a puffy fish. The blood dark, almost black. Why this desire to record my period? Why do I feel the need to tell my friends "I've got it," and to complain about my cramps, even though they're not that bad? Does it make me feel more womanly? Daring—to mention the unmentionable?

I feel inadequate right now, and full of longing. Have a need for control right now; need to control each day as it appears. Prefer waking to falling asleep. Should go on a diet. Perhaps eat nothing but apples. Judith brought me a bunch of fresh picked ones: delicious, crisp green.

October 19. New Hampshire

Menstruation seems private to me this month. I don't want to share it, or write about it.

Exhilarated.

November 15. New Hampshire

Got my period walking uphill from town. Wetness between the labia. Stella and Jackie stopped and gave me a ride. It was good to have someone to complain to: "Oh! I just got my period!" Even told Scott at dinner. But as V. says: "Are you boasting or complaining?"

A month of chastity. Took a hot bath—no cramps to speak of. A white month. No one demanding my body for an entire cycle. No sperm to wash off. Celibacy is so quiet, so still. Perfect for this time of year when life goes underground. Menstruating now just before the new moon. A new beginning.

December 14. New Hampshire

The world covered lightly in snow. The birches, the evergreens, newly revealed by the white blanket, seeming even more perfectly themselves. I imagine a drop of blood in the snow—like Snow White's mother who pricked her finger and let three drops fall on whiteness. Bleeding, bleeding, the body comes round again and again, dying a small death, giving birth to a whole self again.

January 14, 1980. Boston

Menstruating. As if I were a torso of marble, a marble woman without arms. My belly hard and cold. Inside, a transparent glass of blood turned upside down and blood running down and out and down my legs for days. I have no arms to stop it. What do arms do? They embrace, lift, take; my hands write. The suicide tells me she wants to cut off her hands because they have hurt someone. My arms have hurt no one but myself; arms that keep reaching out, begging for love. I want my arms back. With arms, I can reach up into myself and staunch the flow of blood as it still flows.

BLEEDING TO DEATH
Sherry Lee

I always get "crazy"
when I bleed.

As if all the years,
the centuries
of oppression
swell up inside me.

Then painfully push/out
expelling
the stench
of ancient
garbage.

In 1981, in England, Christine English was acquitted of murdering her lover because her PMS turned her into "a raging animal each month."[35] The English press had a heyday with this trial, with its implication that all women are potentially unreliable.[36] Christine English's motives for killing this man, and what he had done to provoke her, were ignored; her motive, her reason, was reduced to PMS.[37]

This defense, although good for Christine English, is harmful to women in general. It takes us back to the statement made by Hubert Humphrey's physician that a woman couldn't be president because of her "raging hormonal imbalance."[38] It provides the male establishment with an excuse to keep women out of positions of power and responsibility, and even for discrediting women as witnesses in court,[39] by claiming the possibility of being "crazy" with PMS. This popular theme may result in a spate of books and movies on the subject of women driven crazy by PMS, a skewed and dangerous view rebutted by Nadine Brozan in an article in the *New York Times*.

> Only 5% are said to experience it [PMS] with such severity that they are forced to curtail their activities, and those who...are capable of harmful behavior...represent a tiny fraction of the serious syndrome sufferers.[40]

It is true, however, that most women do have some form of PMS, even if it is just breast tenderness. But we are labelled 'deviant' when compared to the male body which does not go through a reproductive cycle and is considered the "norm." Thus, women's changes in their bodies and emotions are called "problems," and must therefore be treated.

As Ellen Goodman writes:

> ...women and the female cycle are often regarded as "abnormal" but it is still by and large men who define normal, even while committing 90% of the crimes and waging nearly all the wars.[41]

A double standard exists. Everyone is aware that men's moods change, but a man does not need to explain his temper tantrums and male violence is accepted as part of their nature. (The traditional wifely role was to placate men's moods.) Women's violence, however, goes against the accepted view of the feminine.[42] PMS is now cited as the cause, and female frustration can continue to be ignored or invalidated; drugs are given to soothe the women and ensure they are not disruptive.

> There's no evidence that women are in fact more unpredictable or inconsistent than men—it's a stereotype that men like to encourage.[43]

The history of PMS, says Sophie Laws in *Seeing Red,* should be viewed politically. The current popularity of PMS might well be linked to the resurgence of the women's liberation movement.[44] In the final analysis, it is just another way of keeping women down.

Looking Into the Pain

> It seems very likely that a few women do have some kind of disorder (or some kind of disorders) of the menstrual cycle which really is abnormal, just as there is some group of people with problems in every organ or system in the body. The problem with nearly all the existing work on PMT is that it has no clear conception of what a normal woman, complete with normal menstrual cycle changes, is like. They work instead with sexist stereotypes. Useful "scientific evidence" will not emerge while the scientists hold such twisted views of their "subjects."[45]

Menstrual pain, physical and emotional, is real. We have doubled over with it. We have felt tremendously depressed and unloved. Why should a normal, cyclical function be so hard on us and uncomfortable? There is little else our bodies normally do regularly that causes distress. Birth and death are quite possibly painful, but they are not recurring. Consider childbirth, a natural bodily activity that is also, like menstruation, considered to be painful. However, we know that "painless" childbirth exists. Some women who have "gone into" the pain, breathed with it, "become it" have described births without the agonizing pain commonly associated with childbirth. Also, we have examples from other cultures of painless childbirth.

If this is possible with birthing, might we not dive deeper into menstrual pain and irritability to see what it is and use it in some positive way? In presenting this possibility, there is no intent to belittle menstrual pain or suggest it would all go away with a better attitude. Yet, some of us can benefit by looking closely at the upsets, rage, and sense of 'worthlessness' that often accompany PMS. We can ask ourselves what these worthless feelings have to say about women's position in society. If we are more sensitive and responsive in the pre-menstrual phase, then perhaps we realize, even unconsciously, that what bothers us is very important to us. We can't just brush it off as we usually do the rest of the month; it erupts in the classic PMS symptoms because, pre-menstrually, feelings we've repressed all month characteristically surface.

Even if women agree with Susan Brownmiller that menstruation is a "nasty inconvenience," we need to realize that menstruation differentiates us from men. Menstruation connects women to the larger cycles of birth and death, it opens us up, it gentles us. This very cyclicity is seen as threatening by our linear society. Women who want to be "successful" in this society must ignore it.

> Even the periodicity itself, the inexorable regularity of a cycle that runs like clockwork, is an order of disorder, a disruption of the everyday routine, an imposition of cautious caretaker concerns...it forces women to pay minute attention to the inner workings of the body in a way that men find difficult to comprehend.[46]

Some women are more energetic, if restless, before and during their periods, and are able to use this time creatively in various ways such as writing, painting, thinking things out, gardening, and generally making strides in their work.

— I get much more introspective and mind-oriented so in one way I'm much more energetic (psychic) but physical energy is less.

— High, overhigh. I want to do too much. Very creative.

— I often feel high energy premenstrually.

This nervous tension, this energy and rushing about, is a "symptom" particularly upsetting to husbands. There is always the assumption, one writer says, that it is the *woman* who is "out of tune" and who must change her behavior.[47]

> Hope the blood comes soon. I want to stop being afraid. I am coming apart, breaking in two, the usual inner chatter has turned to shrieking: blind power. What could I do with this power? Do I even *want* this power? (From "Blood Dreams" by Claudia Frei)

The changes that women experience can be transformed into power that will enrich our lives. We needn't fear these changes. They are a part of our cycle, and we must no longer be ashamed of them. The intensity, the sensitivity of this time of menstruation can enhance our creativity and can make us aware of what is not right in our lives.

Judy Grahn has said:

> I try to spend time by myself because I feel pleasantly introverted and a little spaced-out (or in)...Often this state includes strong feelings of renewed purposefulness to life, self-respect, and good will and gentleness toward other beings.[48]

Certainly women go through hormonal changes associated with menstruation. Lynda Birke and Katy Gardner, in *Why Suffer?* suggest that it's how we *perceive* these changes that's important. If we feel somehow "different," and believe—because of everything we've heard—that we're probably going to be irritable, depressed, etc., then we're likely to interpret the hormonal changes as such. However, if we feel positive about menstruation, we might interpret this premenstrual arousal as elation and joy.[49]

One PMS counselor encourages women to use their premenstrually-heightened emotional energy in creative pursuits, and to become familiar with the feelings that come up, ones which are usually kept below the surface. "In a very real way, women are lucky to have this special time"[50]

> If one can accept what one is shown at such a time...one's fear is likely to diminish, and so are the physical reactions....new gifts and startling energies are there for the taking.[51]

7: Menstrual Blood

VARIATIONS IN RED

Marion Cohen

Droplets of rose wine on the toilet paper one morning
Fragments of a timid sunset
rose-colored glasses and magenta food coloring
herald my new week.
A host of red shadows signal the evening's fall
 ballet-costume red, cotton-candy-red, tracing-paper-red, Indian-gauze-fabric-red, pink-red, sky-blue-pink-red, pap-smear-red
soon relax into plain ol' red-red.
Mae-West's-lips-red, orange-yellow-red, fire-engine-
 motor-cycle-siren-red, fresh-blazing-saddles-red, a child's favorite color red
fingernail-polish-red, C-major-red
I-am-here-red.
See my red badge of courage?
Layer upon layer of red oil
gathering in the street.
Pile upon pile of soothing salve
tiny buckets of red rain.
Thinning out, now
A times-are-scarce-red,
A dark red, brown red, brick red, ocean red,
crackly red, wound red
sands of auburn rocks.
The everpresent red you see when you close your eyes
 tight.
Then a fading red, the last red, white red.

Red, red woman's blood. Australian aborigines painted themselves and their sacred objects with red ochre, and called it menstrual blood. The Maori considered blood color to be magic, and they made objects sacred by coloring them red, saying it was menstrual blood. Andaman Islanders painted sick people with blood-red paint, a powerful medicine. Funeral furnishings and graves reddened with ochre, to resemble the Earth Mother's womb "from which the dead could be 'born again'" can be traced in Greece and southern Russia as far back as Paleolithic times.[1]

The Greeks called menstrual blood "supernatural red wine" and gave it to their gods. In India, Kali, the goddess of rebirth, invited gods "to bathe in the bloody flow of her womb and to drink of it; and the gods, in holy communion, drank of the fountain of life...and bathed in it, and rose blessed to the heavens."[2]

> "The Norse god Thor...reached the magic land of enlightenment and eternal life by bathing in a river filled with the menstrual blood of 'giantesses'.[3]

Until the 18th century it was widely believed that menstrual blood retained in a woman's body was the substance of babies. Aristotle spoke of humans being made from a 'coagulum' of menstrual blood. Pliny wrote that menstrual blood could form into a substance which could "groweth to the form of a body."[4]

Today, however, most of us are ashamed of this blood. We are terrified it will show on our clothing and disgrace us. Much time and energy is given to hiding this blood and removing it from our clothes and bedding. We buy products that "protect"—protect us, protect our clothing, protect others from knowing we are bleeding.

— Blood stains on the sheets seem inevitable. Once after making love while I was bleeding, we noticed that the blood and sperm had made a beautiful pattern on the sheet. We cut it out, framed it, and set it on a dresser. Period Art. When my mother came over, she said, "What's that! Blood?" She knew. We all know. I thought about making a soft red pad to use when making love while bleeding— maybe an infant's water-proof pad covered with red velvet. Or maybe a red plush pillow. In the meantime, we bought beige sheets with brown and orange flowers on them.[5]

REMOVING STAINS

Nancy Shiffrin

I picture the woman whose moon-blood this is, her legs in the air, calling your name. Katharine, puckered lips, wispy hair? I see her tottering down the steps, wrapped in her purple shawl, just a chum now, you said. Did you feed her truffles at 2:00 A.M.? You should have soaked the sheets in cold water right away!

The girdle Mama gave me at first sign cut my thighs, protected the mattress. She'd shake me awake at midnight, poke me to see that I kept it on. Hebrew tradition forbids menstruating woman taking meals with family. She may not touch food, utensils, plates. Sex at that time sin. Punishment death for husband and wife.

Forgive? Dissolve the yellow residue? Love in Christ? Once Zada took me to see a kosher butchering, swift slice, thorough draining. Mama still feels under my nightgown, by that dream I know when I'm due. You and Katharine and I picnic in the sunlight, a red-checkered tablecloth spread on the ground. She offers me wine, you drink from the cup. I describe my observances, the pains I take to keep from soiling the bed.

WEDDING 1929

Mary Sue Koeppel

Three months before her wedding
She couldn't ruin her hands with water -
Her mother's wish

So her sister monthly
Washed her bloody rags by hand -
Elbow deep in water

She soaked, bleached
Rubbed with yellow soap
Rinsed away the clots

That sister never married
Never stained man nor woman's hand
With blood.

In an attempt to honor menstruation and to raise their own consciousness, the authors of *The Curse* held a "bleed-in" with their friends. They decorated the bathroom with menstrual paraphernalia, sat in a circle and told stories of their first period (some for the first time). They drank Bloody Marys and laughed and began to tear away the shame and repression that surrounds menstrual blood. They wanted to change their attitude toward menstruation, and to pass this new feeling on to their daughters.[6]

When my youngest daughter started her periods, she caused some amusement around our house. I had been taught, and have continued, to wrap up the used pads before throwing them into the waste basket, and my oldest daughter did likewise. The youngest, however, cavalierly tossed them away "as is" for all to see. As the author of a book celebrating menstruation, I couldn't very well ask her to hide the evidence! So we had a discussion and a good laugh about it, and she continued to do it. Not only that, she took a clean pad, colored it with red pen, wrote "used" on it, and stuck it up on the refrigerator door. It showed up in different parts of the house until the stickiness wore off the back, and we giggled about it when visitors came. (No one said a word!) Perhaps she was making fun of me and this book, but at least she was not ashamed or felt she needed to hide the fact that she was menstruating.

Some women wear red on days they are bleeding, perhaps as a way of announcing their menstruation to those who might notice:

— I celebrate my period by wearing red clothes. Wearing rose oil perfume. Wearing my red tiger-eye ring. I mark it by pressing the mouth of a tube of acrylic paint to the days on the calendar, making blood-red half-moons.

— Sometimes I wear red and take myself to the movies or to lunch.

— Often, I know when I am going to begin menstruation because that day by seeming chance, I put on something red. I am conscious during my period of choosing red to wear, joyfully, flaunting my altered state.[7]

Absorbing it, Catching it, Letting it Flow

The methods of catching menstrual blood depended traditionally on what was readily available. American Indian women used bird down, cattail down, moss, buckskin, rolled buffalo hair, soft buffalo skin, shredded bark, and sheep pelts.[8] Egyptian women in the 15th century used soft papyrus tampons.[9] Sponges were used by women living close to the sea. Many of our mothers and grandmothers used rags.

Disposable towels were developed as early as 1886 but could not be marketed because advertising such a product was considered immoral. In 1921 gauze Kotex was manufactured, and then advertised in *The Ladies Home Journal* in 1924.[10] Tampons were first put on the market in 1936. Today, "feminine protection" is a huge industry, with an $850 million/year market; $60 million is spent annually on advertising tampons.[11]

Nancy Friedman, author of *Everything You Must Know About Tampons,* thinks women should challenge this industry, in fact, take it over. This is starting to happen on a small scale, particularly with re-usable menstrual pads and sponges. "Menstrual products are women's concern," she says. "It's time to make them women's business as well."[12]

For millions of women, tampons are associated with freedom and comfort. Initially, they appeared to be a safe method of absorbing menstrual blood, but changes were later made in the composition of tampons and types of inserters that constituted in some cases health hazards for women.

Plastic inserters were introduced in the 60s, and petal-tipped plastic inserters with sharp points came out in the early 70s. Deodorant tampons were first marketed in 1969. Then, in the mid-70s, technology made it possible to manufacture super-absorbent tampons whose thirsty fibers were first used in the agriculture industry on seeds and soil to increase water retention, then put to use by tampon manufacturers. They are also used in sanitary pads and diapers.[13]

By 1980, 70% of all American women used tampons at some time in their lives, and they were wearing them between as well as during periods.[14] The advertisers tell women it is not nice to leak, anything, ever.

And then reports of problems started coming in. First there were reports of vaginal ulcerations in 1977. By the summer of 1980, toxic shock syndrome was front-page news, but the cause was unknown. Ninety-five percent of TSS victims are females between the ages of 15 and 34; 70% of these were wearing tampons when stricken.[15] Tampons were suspected, but no one knew why. By the end of 1980, 115 lawsuits had been filed, and every tampon manufacturer except Purex (Pursettes) sued at least once.[16]

Tampon manufacturers are not required by law to list ingredients or perform safety tests.[17] In the mid-70s, health activists tried to find out what was in tampons, and were told by the manufacturers that the information was "proprietary." Rely tampons, now off the market because of their association with toxic shock syndrome, originally contained polymethene, a carcinogen.[18]

The FDA first recognized in 1981 that there was a link between higher absorbency and toxic shock syndrome, and in August of 1987 an article in the *Journal of the American Medical Association* stated again that it is the absorbency of the tampons, not the chemical composition, which is the main cause of TSS.[19]

The least absorbent tampons are Tampax Junior and Regular. The most absorbent are Kotex Super and OB Super. Since there are "regulars" that are more absorbent than some "supers," it can be confusing for the consumer. According to 1983 absorbency ratings, Playtex regulars were more absorbent than Tampax and Kotex supers.[20]

A letter from the National Women's Health Network, February 1988, states that the FDA has proposed regulations for tampon absorbency labeling, but it has not as yet been approved at the departmental level. "The proposed regulations would mandate that all tampons be subjected to a uniform test for absorbency. A numerical range gauging the number of grams of fluid absorbed by the tampon, similar to the ranking system for sunscreens, will assure that all tampons can be compared."

Tampon packaging now provides information about TSS. Symptoms include: fever of 102 degrees or higher, vomiting, diarrhea, dizziness, fainting, a sunburn-like rash, and a sudden drop in blood pressure. If you have these symptoms and are wearing a tampon, *take it out!* Then call a doctor or go to an emergency facility immediately. People who receive immediate and proper treatment usually recover in two to three weeks.

There are other problems with tampons besides TSS. Retrograde menstruation (menstruation going backwards because the flow is blocked) may cause severe cramps and endometriosis.[21] The tampon string can act as a wick for carrying bacteria from the anus into the vagina. Plastic inserters may tear vaginal walls. Tampon fibers may be left behind in the vagina. Fragrance materials may be harmful.

If you must wear tampons, check the absorbency, bearing in mind that greater absorbency is associated with TSS. As explained, there is no set absorbency rating, and tampon manufacturers may change the absorbency of a tampon at any time. Your local women's health center may have an up-to-date listing. Change tampons frequently (every 2-6 hours) but not too often (or they'll be too dry to remove without chafing). Use pads at night and on light days. Don't wear tampons unless you are menstruating. Avoid all deodorized tampons; they are unnecessary, because menstrual blood is odorless until it comes in contact with bacteria in the air. If you use tampons with plastic applicators, be sure the tampon is all the way inside so the flaps do not pinch or scratch the vagina. *Look* at them—take them apart, put them in water to see whether they come apart.[22]

Some women make their own tampons from sterile cotton or gauze. One uses two or three cotton balls at a time. Strings are not necessary.

In considering the tampon issue, Emily Culpepper made a film called *Period Piece* which dissects attitudes toward menstrual blood. She believes that tampons encourage us to hide our periods. For example, the tampon ads show women wearing white so that "no one will know." In this culture, blood shed in violence is more acceptable than menstrual blood; hiding the menses has become a profitable obsession.[23]

A MENSTRUATION POEM

Lisa Larges

I used to have bad dreams
about staining my clothes;
It used to be a preoccupation in me,
how to save myself from being found out.
And it was all shame and secret,
the toilet, the garbage, the dirty tampons
wrapped in white toilet paper.
The clean tampons hidden away.

My sister stained her wedding dress.
It was not her time, as the women would say,
but it was the sign of her fear, which she could not tell.
My mother, my sister, myself,
there in the bathroom, the three of us,
i felt in me a primal terror.

But now i am wanting a new dream;
consulting with the dream mistress to get rid of Freud;
and the new dream could be:
Walking, and letting the warm blood leave my body,
sticking to the hair on my legs,
splattering on the warm earth, staining the cold cement,
turning the snow to crimson,
a spot of life on the death of things.

Take out your tampon my love,
this will be our manifesto;
We shall not be stopped
A conspiracy with the moon, and the earth, and the ocean,
with the great river of life, and the Goddess.
And in our revolution we shall say, This is my body, this is
my blood.

Some women believe a sponge is the ideal material for absorbing menstrual blood.

> Natural sponges are advantageous over tampons for many reasons. First, they are reusable and therefore ecological. Secondly, we aren't supporting a huge and, no doubt, polluting industry when we rinse out our own sponges. This is a good way to get "in touch" with your periods. Handling your sponge and blood helps to discharge lots of our self-disgust, so inculcated by media, myths and poor health. You have an opportunity to *smell* your blood....Blood will cease to "freak you out."[24]

The disadvantages of sponges are that they may leak, and they may contain harmful chemicals. One woman was told by her doctor that her vaginal infection was caused by the iodine in the sponge she was using. Traces of hydrocarbons, possibly from an oil spill, were found in one sample of sponges.[25] In a 1980 study sponges contained bacteria, fortunately not Staphylococcus aureus, the bacterium associated with toxic shock syndrome.[26]

In 1980, the FDA declared sponges to be unapproved medical devices, a dictum that slowed down their advertising and distribution. Some women's health centers are suspicious of the FDA's interest in sponges, since sponges are a potential rival to the tampon industry. Only two cases of TSS have been associated with sponges, a lower incidence of TSS than in men and young children.[27]

The "Report on TSS - March 1981" by the Boston Women's Health Book Collective says:

> More research needs to be done on the safety of sponges for menstruation. There are mixed reports on whether sponges are contaminated by pollutants while growing in the ocean and how serious a problem this is....The Food and Drug Administration is harassing the sponge distributors, usually one-woman businesses, to get them to stop selling sponges, while moving slowly in requiring stricter standards for tampons.
>
> To use a sponge, tie a piece of strong string or dental floss around it or through one end. Dampen it before insertion. A sponge holds about as much as a tampon or napkin. When you think the sponge is full, pull the string to remove it. Wash it well in cool water and soap, which is sufficient to kill bacteria. Before re-inserting it, squeeze it in a towel to remove excess water. The sponge does not have to be made sterile....tampons and napkins are not sterile. To make things simpler in public restrooms, you can carry an extra sponge in a small plastic bag. Sponges with small holes absorb more. If the sponge seems too large, cut it to the right size for you. "Silk" sponges are available at cosmetic counters or fancy soap displays. "Elephant ear" sponges are available in pottery and art supply stores.[28]

Other women have written that the strings are unnecessary; sponges are quite easy to remove with fingers. A woman from Arizona wrote that she washes hers with vinegar, not soap, and sets it "picturesquely on the branches of a piece of coral to dry." She also says,

> ...true, sponges require more care than commercial tampons—and home cooking takes more effort than tv dinners...sponges bring us closer to what is really going on with our bodies...we learn that menstrual blood neither smells bad nor is offensive to touch...we see its colors as we haven't before, when we cleanse our sponges—ruby and garnet hues flowing into the stream of water.[29]

If we use pads rather than tampons, which in a sense hide our blood from us, we of necessity have a different relationship with our blood. We see it and we smell it. Every time we go to the bathroom we know exactly what is happening with our period.

A few women, not wanting to support the "sanitary products" industry and wanting to be more involved with their blood, make their own pads.

> — There is a political concern in purchasing pre-packaged sanitary napkins. We support a gigantic industry that perpetuates images of powerless, pretty ladies – and equates "whiteness" with purity. Let's make our own![30]

Make pads out of cotton, wool, or silk (natural materials). "Note what color you feel like wearing...No one said you have to wear white."[31]

The most important aspect of this process—"making your own"—is the sense of self-worth and appreciation you bring to this ritual. Creating a receptacle for your blood is a positive affirmation of your femaleness and is to be celebrated.[32] (Parvati gives instructions on how to make your own menstrual pads on pp. 15-16 of *Hygieia*. See Appendix II, Resources & Readings.)

Other women have written:

— I like the sensation of blood flowing (one reason I prefer napkins) and feel tuned into myself.

— I make my own pads—soak out the sacred blood—give that blood to plants in my own garden—give thanks. Special bleedings, like first post-partum menses, I use red silk covered pads, but usually old diapers—sometimes 'Glad Rags.'

— I've made my own pads-they are white flannel with tiny red flowers on them-it feels special to care for my own pads-I love it![33]

Diaphragms and cervical caps are sometimes used to collect blood. As with tampons, they should not be left in too long. The BWHBC says, "The diaphragm holds a lot more than a sponge or tampon. When you think it is full, remove it, wash it out, and re-insert. To make insertion easier, you can apply birth control cream, jelly or K-Y Jelly to the rim."[34]

Another product, the menstrual cup, was sold in U.S. between early 1950s and 1972 before the manufacturer went bankrupt. Designed by a ballet dancer and her physician husband, it was called "Tassette" - French for "little cup". It was widely praised by women users and doctors who tested the device as safe, clean, convenient. Tassettes did not injure vaginal walls, had less bacterial contamination than pads or tampons, and held a lot of blood so even women with heavy flows could use them. The problem was that the company was not making money because a single cup lasted 10 years or longer. "Tassaway" - a disposable cup - was developed in 1968. Women liked this product very much, but the company lost money in advertising and couldn't afford to continue manufacturing "Tassaways."[35]

Some women don't use anything to stop their blood. Women have written telling me they let the blood run freely outdoors, particularly in their gardens.

ROSIE

Janet Aalfs

An old Eskimo woman once said:
"If you let the blood run
you will make yourself better.
If there are spirits that want to leave
they will leave with the blood."
—Anonymous

Rosie doesn't like Tampax.
They weave asbestos into the threads
to make us bleed,
to make us buy more.
The thought of all that blood
stuck in a wad of paper
shoved up our vaginas is repulsive, unnatural.
Dylis reminds us of her mother who had to use rags.
She rinsed them out in cold water.
Tampax meant no more cold hands four times a day
or blood-specked washbasins.
Funny how times change
Beth uses a sponge.
She revels in the rush of red
as she squeezes it under the faucet.
How it gives like her own insides.
Keeps giving.
The odor after three days is not sweet.
Stale blood, old tissue.
Rosie wants to pull the plug.
Bleed all over banks and sidewalks.
Leave permanent stains on carpets and sofas.
So they can't hide from the sight or smell of it.
Or make money off it.
She wants all us women to stop crossing our legs,
pursing our lips.
So the spirits that want can leave with the blood.
To make ourselves better.

Mary Beth Edelson has these comments from women in her "Menstruation Stories":[36]

> I like my blood to flow naturally around my vulva and legs. It is so nice to forget about tampons and underwear; I pretend I am a native woman, smelling and touching my body blood.

It is my own private world, but I would like to meet other tribal women to share this rite.

TAMPONS

Ellen Bass

My periods have changed. It is years
since I have swallowed pink and gray darvons, round
chalky midols from the bottle with the smiling girl.
Now I plan a quiet space,
protect myself those first few days when my uterus lets
go and I am an open anemone. I know
when my flow will come. I watch my mucous pace
changes like a dancer, follow the fall
and rise of my body heat. All this
and yet I never questioned them, those slim white
handies.

It took me years to learn to use them
starting with pursettes and a jar of vaseline.
I didn't even know where the hole was.
I didn't even know enough
to try to find one. I pushed until
only a little stuck out and hoped
that was far enough.
I tried every month through high school.

And now that I can change it in a moving car—
like Audrey Hepburn changing dresses in the taxi
in the last scene of Breakfast at Tiffany's—
I've got to give them up.

Tampons, I read, are
bleached, are
chemically treated to
compress better,
contain asbestos.
Good old asbestos. Once we learned not to shake it—
Johnson & Johnson's—on our babies or diaphragms,
we thought we had it licked.

So what do we do? They're universal.
Even macrobiotics and lesbian separatists are hooked on
them
Go back to sanitary napkins?
Junior high, douple napkins

on the heavy days, walking home damp underpants
chafing thighs. It's been a full twelve years
since I have worn one, since Spain
when Marjorie pierced my ears
and I unloaded half a suitcase of the big gauze
pads in the hotel trash.

Someone in my workshop suggested tassaways, little
cups that catch the flow.
They've stopped making them,
we're told. Women found they could reuse them
and the company couldn't make enough
money that way. Besides,
the suction pulled the cervix out of shape.

Then diaphragms.
It presses on me, one woman says.
So swollen those days. Too tender.

Menstrual extraction, a young woman says.
I heard about that. Ten minutes
and it's done.
But I do not trust putting tubes into my uterus each
month.
We're told everything is safe
in the beginning.

Mosses.
The Indians used mosses.
I live in Aptos. We grow
succulents and pine.
I will buy mosses
when they sell it at the co-op

Okay. It's like the whole birth control schmear.
There just isn't a good way. Women bleed.
We bleed.
The blood flows out of us. So we will bleed.
Blood paintings on our thighs, patterns
like river beds, blood on the chairs in
insurance offices, blood on Greyhound buses
and 747's, blood blots, flower forms
on the blue skirts of stewardesses.
Blood on restaurant floors, supermarket aisles,
the steps of government buildings.
Sidewalks

will have

blood trails,

like

Gretel's bread

crumbs. We can always find our way.
We will start to recognize each other by smell.
We will ease into rhythm together, it happens
when women live closely—African tribes, college
  sororities—
our blood flowing on the same days. The first day
of our heaviest flow we will gather in Palmer,
  Massachusetts
on the steps of Tampax, Inc. We'll have a bleed-in.
We'll smear the blood on our faces. Max Factor
will join OB in bankruptcy. The perfume
industry will collapse, who needs
whale sperm, turtle oil, when we have free blood?
For a little while cleaning products will boom,
409, Lysol, Windex. But
the executives will give up. The cleaning woman is leaving a
red wet rivulet, as she scrubs down the previous stains.
It's no use. The men would have to
do it themselves, and that will never come up
for a vote at the Board.
Women's clothing manufacturers, fancy
furniture, plush carpet all will phase out. It's just not
practical. We will live the old ways.

Simple floors, dirt or concrete, can be hosed down
or straw, can by cycled through the compost.
Simple clothes, none in summer. No more swimming
  pools.
Swim in the river. Yes, swim in the river.
Dogs will fall in love with us.
We'll feed the fish with our blood. Our blood
will neutralize the chemicals and dissolve the old car
  parts.
Our blood will detoxify the phosphates and the
PCB's. Our blood will feed the depleted soils.
Our blood will water the dry, tired surface of the earth.
We will bleed. We will bleed. We will
bleed until we bathe her in our blood and she turns
slippery new like a baby birthing.

Menstrual extraction is a process of removing all the menstrual blood of a woman's period in 5 to 15 minutes. It is done by inserting a suction tube called a cannula into the uterus. It was developed by women at the Self-Help Clinic of the Feminist Women's Health Center in Los Angeles.[37]

The writers of *The Curse* who are very enthusiastic about this technique say it is revolutionary, quick, inexpensive, and simple: "the most advanced development in monthly protection." They also believe it gives a woman complete control of her body. If a woman's period is late and she is worried about pregnancy, menstrual extraction is a way of performing an abortion.[38]

Menstrual extraction, at this point, is controversial from three angles: health, legal, and political. From the point of view of women's health, it is possible that this technique is not completely safe and may cause infections and damage to the uterus. Legally, there are questions about whether the procedure constitutes an abortion and practicing medicine without a license. And politically, some wonder who actually will be controlling women's bodies if menstrual extraction is performed, and who will reap the profits from the potentially saleable item used in the procedure.

Nora Ephron has an interesting comment on menstrual extraction:

> For some time, various scientists have been attacking women's liberation by insisting that because of menstruation, women are unfit for just about everything several days a month. In a way, the Los Angeles (Self-Help Clinic) women are supporting this assertion in their use of period extraction for non-abortion purposes; what they are saying, in effect, is yes, it *is* awful, it is truly a curse, and here is a way to be done with it in five minutes.[39]

PERIOD POEM
Deborah S. Abbott

Five hundred twenty one days
since that familiar ache
in the hollowed palm of pelvis;
since that throb which,
like the pulsing of a new bruise,
grows warm and tender to the touch;
since that scarlet flow
coursed the convolutions of vagina
and soaked the cotton between my legs.

Well, come blood,
come down and out of your dark womb,
I am anxious to remember you.
After five hundred twenty one days
I had almost forgotten
how much you taste like the sea,

how much like the sea your saline broth
nourishes and bathes.
I had almost forgotten
how your scent permeates
layers of pad, of pant, of stocking,
of heavy woolen skirt,
how it announces itself
to the woman on the bus bench beside me.
Even as strangers,
this bond of ours as bleeding women.
We smile,
the shame we shared at twelve,
at sixteen, at twenty six—
at twenty eight we share no longer.

After five hundred twenty one days,
o blood,
I want to proclaim you,
to snatch the microphone
from the mouth of the driver
who mumbles only street names.
I want the old man sleeping off
his half-pint to be roused,
to get up out of his seat
even while the bus moves,
to shake my hand and say
"Good for you, dear, good for you.
Hope you don't have to wait
so long for the next."

I want the woman with the wig askew
on her head to hear my news,
and straighten her hair,
and shout all the way to the back
where I'm sitting
"Well, well! Best news I've heard all week.
Remember those glorious days myself."
I want the fourteen year old
who slumps at the other end
of the long, last seat
to slide over and ask
"Got any extra?"
And after scooping up a fingerful,
I want to watch him make brilliant graffiti
with my flow.

Welcome, blood,
Come back again soon.
No more babies for a while;
even a daughter can wait.
I need you more than I need her.
I need every drop of you,
every pungent, clotted drop.
I need to cycle,
to let out my breath
and take it in,
as the body invites even winter
to break the course of fall.
After five hundred twenty one days
without release,
as though the moon
had a magnet's grip on my womb,
turning blood to stone,
I need to cycle.
Pity men, their relentless path,
I welcome this blood-letting,
this letting go.

A PERIOD OF QUIET BUT COLOURFUL PROTEST

Joan Fern Shaw

Again she felt the warm oozing. Yes, it would be through the white skirt by now. Red on white. Like the flag. But that's blasphemy. Still, there's the poppy for Remembrance Day. Isn't the red supposed to stand for blood?...

Everyone had left the bus but Mary. The driver turned around.

"Ma'am, this is the end of the line."

Yes, oh prophetic one, it certainly is.

Mary was glued to the seat. If only she could stand up and walk. Then the whole thing would be started, underway. Another dribble. Running down her leg. The new pearlnet panty-hose. Still, blood doesn't stain permanently. Soak in cold water.

Mary rose from her single seat without looking back. She walked to the front of the bus where the door was still open. A breeze smelling oddly of popcorn ruffled the transfer pad. Pad. The protest movement. She wished the driver would stop looking at her but that was part of it. People had to look.

"Uh, Ma'am...I think, uh, you've had," he cleared his throat, "a little accident."

Well, this is it.

"No, it's not an accident. I mean, I know what I'm doing." If she didn't get her point across now, she never would. Was one of his eyes a darker blue than the other? She tried to remember the speech she'd rehearsed with the tape recorder. "You see, I'm protesting against the sales tax on sanitary supplies. Like napkins, belts, tampons...those new things, uh, liners...that sort of thing. It's not fair to put a tax on them because..." Mary's face was as scarlet as the blotch on the back of the skirt. It's so much easier in the middle of the night with a tape recorder... "...so I thought if I made a public display maybe other women would join in and we'd..." It had seemed brilliant when she thought about it at home in bed. Alone. Every night since Jim had left her. She had always accepted everything, even that. Without protest. After all those years of working so Jim could finish school, putting off having a family, putting off getting her own degree. Then he left. As Momma would have said, he up-and-left-her. Always up. Up, in contrast to her down. Mary the Doormat. Lie there and get stepped on. But not now. Now she was finally taking a stand. Of sorts.

The bus driver was staring at her flaming face, searching over his experiences with the tired, the irritated, the drunk, the confused, the sick. He'd seen them all...

"Okay, I can see your point. About the tax. But what about the next passenger that sits in your seat? Say it's a poor old fellow wearing his Sunday best on the way to meet a nice lady friend for lunch. And he doesn't see too well, so he sits in that." He pointed the the seat she'd just left. The green vinyl was smeared with blood, swirls and dots, a grotesque finger-painting in Christmas colours.

"Well, I thought that sort of thing would help to prove my point. Like a strike. Someone has to get hurt to drive the message home, you see. Well, like your bus strike. I had to walk twelve blocks to work but it sort of proved you were essential or at least necessary. I got blisters on both feet. So, if all the women join in all over the city, there'll be blood on seats in restaurants, movie theatres...and then everyone will see that sanitary supplies are essential for society..." She gulped air.

"Okay, but did you have to start with my bus?" He was smiling at her. The darker eye was more hooded than the other and it sort of winked at her. But it wasn't a put-down smile. There was a fleck of something else. Admiration, maybe? No, surely not.

"Well, yes, I suppose the person...the poor old man going to visit his...I suppose he would just give you the flack if he sits in my...in that. I haven't figured it all out yet." She took out a purse-sized package of tissues and began to soak up the blood. "I've got to get the details worked out. Get my act together, I guess it's called." She continued to blot away at the smear.

The driver unfolded himself from his seat and came toward her with a yellow J-Cloth inside a plastic baggy...

He put the bus into gear. "Do you want to stay on and go back home? You won't have to pay another fare. You didn't get off." He still had the yellow cloth in his hand.

"No." Her voice was weak with indecision. "I'm going on with it." It was almost a question.

"Lady, the best of luck." His words came out with a force that surprised her. "And let me tell you something. You've got guts!"

After a few seconds they both laughed at the significance of the words and Mary waved her red Kleenex as proof. He held out his hand. "Trevor's the name and let me tell you I think you've got something I wish more people had." His hand was warm and tanned. She was conscious of hers, icy, wet, pale...

"I'm Mary." When her hand slid out of his grasp he didn't wipe off all the sweat she'd left behind. That was nice.

He gave a little shrug and handed her the J-Cloth. "Here, Mary, you may need this again today."

As she stepped out of the bus, she felt another gush. A drop of blood on the cement...Another drop of blood on the floor inside the station. Most of the people hurried by, paying no attention to her. From somewhere below came the screech of a subway train...

"Oh look, that lady's cut her bum." A child's clear soprano. The Emperor's New Clothes. Eyes fastened on her back, her front. Blood was seeping through the front now, too. Heavy flow this month, probably nerves; she made the mental note which was extinguished by the staggering reality. My God, what was she doing? Stepping onto an escalator in a public place, bleeding all over her white linen suit.

She tried to screen the front stain with her purse. And just at that moment, as her body moved below the line of huge windows, she caught sight of the bus driver, pulling up to the two lines of his next load. He saluted her and mouthed something that must have been, "Good luck." Then he pointed frantically to something, someone near the front of the line. She caught a glimpse of a nicely dressed elderly gentleman carrying a bouquet of roses.

She slipped her purse back onto her shoulder and straightened her back...

A tall woman with soft, white hair and a smart blue sundress approached Mary.

"Excuse me, Miss, I think you've got the visitor. There's a washroom just past the candy store..."

The woman put a large hand on Mary's arm. The second big, kind hand today. "Are you all right, dear. Your period's started. I guess 'the visitor' was before your time. I don't have anything with me. Those days are gone, thank heavens. What a nuisance, bleeding one week out of four. There's a machine in the washroom...what is it?...you're not pregnant are you? Shall I call someone?"

"Oh, no. I'm sorry." Mary didn't feel like going through another long explanation about her protest movement. It would be so much easier just to go to the washroom. Maybe rinse the skirt in the toilet bowl and dry it under the hot-air hand dryer. So what if a couple of women saw her in her bloody panty-hose?

But that would be cop-out city...

She told the nice lady about her stand against the tax on sanitary supplies.

"But my dear child, you can't do this all alone. Maybe if you had a club or organisation of some kind behind you." The woman glanced away for a moment, her alert mind sifting through possibilities. Vibrating with ideas. It may have been a subway train underneath, but she seemed to quiver with concentration. Suddenly the lady burst into such a hearty laugh that some of the blank, gaping faces passing by picked up on it and came to life. "All my friends are over the hill too. I can't think of anyone in my circle who could join in your cause, as an active participant. Except my daughter and she wouldn't be seen dead with blood on her precious originals."

Another deep laugh. She gave Mary's arm a pat. They both looked down at Mary's feet where a succession of red drops had formed a tiny puddle. It was the shape of an open rose.

"What an interesting pattern you're making. And it's not your fault. I mean the other...well...excretions. They have muscles and things to hold them back. But this just flows. Like the moon and tides or something. You've presented me with something so new, I can't get it in focus yet. You know, to figure out if it's a stroke of genius or a piece of absurdity."

Adsurdity. It bounced between them. For an instant, the lady lost her composure and the passers-by penetrated with their stares. Mary felt again the blood falling and rising to her face. Shame. Absurdity.

But suddenly the woman looked directly into Mary's eyes and each felt the other's strength returning.

"It's not so much the tax itself, is it dear? It's the affront. I never really thought of it before. Only women have periods."

"Yes, the tax doesn't amount to that much, but there's a principle here. And I had to do something for once in my life."

"Say, I have a bit of influence in the ballet world." She was back in full stride. "Maybe we can talk the female cast of Swan Lake into refusing to wear sanitary protection during the next performances unless the tax is removed. Imagine the spectacle! Odette doing an arabesque in her little white tutu! I think you'll have the support, or at least the sympathy, of most women. But what about the men? My dear, they'll be positively livid. Or will they? I can't think of a precedent. It's not at all the same as burning bras. Look how I'm going on and on. You've really got me excited. Think of the possibilities! But what are your plans? Are you going to carry a sign? You must have a sign."

"Well, I thought a sign would be a bit, uh, brazen. I just thought I'd talk to people. Now I kind of wish I had a sign so I wouldn't have to explain. I had a sort of vague idea of standing around the government buildings, maybe sitting in the visitors' gallery and eating at their cafeteria. There might be some people from the press around. I didn't have a definite plan in mind. I just woke up this morning with my period and I thought now is the time if your're ever going to stand up for anything in your whole life...and I'm on my holidays... You're right. I should have a sign. I've got to get organised. Is there somewhere in the mall where I can buy a piece of bristol board?"

As the two women went off to locate a store, they exchanged names and phone numbers and promised to keep in touch. Emily's parting words to Mary were, "I'll see you on the t.v. news tonight. And watch out, some of us older gals may be joining you...we can always use tomato juice!"

The girl in the office supplies store was calm when she pointed out that Mary was menstruating and yes, they had bristol board at the back of the store. Sex Ed. courses had done a lot to take the blush out of bodily functions, Mary reasoned as she told the girl her plan. The violet-trimmed eyes grew wide and an assortment of earrings jingled from her triple-pierced earlobes. In her excitement, she broke into the current motif, "Awesome, I mean this is totally awesome! It's so decent. I mean this has gotta reach their heads, right? Go for it, Lady. Me and my friends will be totally in there." Or something like that. Mary left the store almost sure that her cause had now received approval from an extremely vocal element of society.

Four microcosms: the working man, the older woman, the teenager and me, Mary the Doormat. If we all think I'm on the right track, then, damn it, maybe I am.

And Mary got down on the floor of the shopping plaza with her sheet of bristol board and her new red magic marker and she printed the first of many, many signs. A little group gathered around her and she explained what she was doing...

...the response to menopause is a function of the woman's pre-menopausal personality and life patterns. The menopause itself does not turn a healthy, functioning woman into an involutional psychotic. - *Pauline Bart*

8: Menopause: Last Blood

We are told that menopause is a terrible time, a crazy time, an illness, signifying the end of a woman's meaningful life. This is what we get from the popular media and from medical references. This is what many doctors believe. However, when women themselves are asked about their menopause, the majority say it was not a bad time. Changes happen, yes. But changes are a part of life, and menopause is a natural process. One woman wrote on the questionnaire:

— Like all stages of life, it is one a woman passes through if she lives long enough. I have not had the usual symptoms of hot flashes or depression. In fact, I compare my body now to the eleven-year-old I was, who waited for the "big event." Now, however, I know it will never return except as a sign of some abnormality (I did have a period after my father's death which I know was an emotional reaction). I dislike the thought it presages "old age."

Pauline Bart's article, "Menopause," affirms that most women do *not* have a hard time during menopause, and of those who do, they generally had those problems before. The studies cited by Bart show that women who are more invested in being 'mothers' (overprotective and overinvolved) have a harder time; that women who are 'invested in sexuality' have an easier time; and that menopause is not perceived as upsetting by women in general.[1]

Why, then, are we presented with such a negative view of menopause? Is this another in the series of attitudes which put women down? Men's changes are not spoken of in such derogatory terms.

When men name their own menopausal condition they do not employ the same vocabulary. Therefore we do not have "testicular insufficiency" to match "ovarian insufficiency," or "senile scrotum" to match "senile ovaries."

Medical books give directions for the "preservation of a serviceable vagina." Do you think there is equal discussion for "serviceable penis?"[2]

Until recently, men have written nearly all the books on menopause, defining it in their own, often misogynist, terms.

Rosetta Reitz, who wrote *Menopause: A Positive Approach,* gave a number of talks on menopause, always introducing herself by saying: "My name is Rosetta Reitz, I'm 50 years old and in my menopause."

She actively sought to dispel the negative attitudes that prevail about menopause by showing she was neither embarrassed nor ashamed of being menopausal herself. When she was to be on TV talking about menopause, Reitz was told she would not have to give her name, and she could be photographed from the back or in shadow so she wouldn't be recognized. "Are you kidding?" she responded. "I'm not ashamed to be identified as a menopausal woman."[3]

She asks, in her book,

Why are the prevailing attitudes about childbirth positive and the ones about menopause negative? What is involved here? Why am I looked on with value when my body is going through one natural function, then, twenty years later, looked on as valueless when my body is going through another natural function? My life changed much more when I became a mother for the first time than when I started to skip periods. It seems to me that "change of life" more accurately describes motherhood than menopause.[4]

In the American mainstream culture, women are valued only when they are young. Paula Weideger says that in this culture women are sexually desirable only when their sexuality also inspires fear, only when they are menstruating. Women are assumed to have lost their sexuality after menopause.[5]

Phyllis Chesler has written:

The savage mockery, the sexual punishment by withdrawal of sexual attention, toward those women who can no longer bear children is partly related to male uterus envy. Once the power of the womb is no longer active, is no longer dangerous, is no longer useful to men, then men can gain some small measure of revenge, men can dare to violate or ignore that which they were forced to court or to trap before. Thus, our tradition of mother-in-law jokes; and the avoidance of "older" women by men, both erotically and spiritually.[6]

Midlife can be a difficult and frustrating time for both sexes, but women particularly are affected by our society's negative attitudes. Menopausal women are not taken seriously, are made to feel invisible, are told their "raging hormones" disqualify them from serious work.

Philip Slater, however, does not agree:

A male bureaucrat once argued that women should not hold positions of responsibility because of the emotional instabilities associated with menopause, but I would rather take my chances with such a woman than with an ordinary power-hungry male. It seems astonishing that we fear menopausal lability more than the icy pathology that allows a man to order massive destruction and the killing and mutilation of hundreds of thousands of people merely to avoid being called weak, or to win points in a game of international chicken.[7]

What Happens at Menopause

The average age of menopause is about 50 (and rising), but as with other aspects of menstruation, it varies enormously. Some women start to feel symptoms at age 35.[8]

Rosetta Rietz says it takes about five years for the menopause to complete itself,[9] but a friend of mine said: "Of all the things I've heard and read about menopause, the only thing that seems true to me is that it takes ten years!"

Our bodies undergo certain changes at menopause. The ovaries produce less and less estrogen, a process which starts slowly in our 20s. The changes in the ovaries affect the other endocrine glands, and our system must readjust to these changes, which may happen unevenly.[10]

Estrogen production slows down but does not stop at menopause; although the ovaries produce less, other glands start producing more. Progesterone, which is produced in the second half of the menstrual cycle to further prepare the uterus for pregnancy, also decreases.[11]

A hysterectomy which includes ovary removal not only ends menstruation but may cause symptoms of menopause. However, if the ovaries—even a part of one—are left in the body, menopausal symptoms will occur as they would have without surgery.[12]

The cessation of menstruation can happen abruptly, gradually, or irregularly. For most women, it happens irregularly, and gets more irregular until menstruation stops altogether. Periods may vary from heavy to scant, long or short, far apart or close together, without any pattern.[13]

Hot flashes are the chief symptom of menopause. It is the one most women talk about, and it is the only symptom consistently found in other cultures. Hot flashes are caused by the blood vessels overdilating in reaction to the chemical and hormonal changes taking place in the body.[14]

Hot flashes vary a great deal. They are usually mild, may be uncomfortable, but are not painful. They generally last a minute or two and occur sporadically: several times an hour, once a day, a few times a month, or very rarely. Hot flashes may happen all through the years of the menopause, even well after the periods have stopped. But, says Reitz, "Most women who experience them—once they have come to accept them—are not very troubled with them."[15]

About half of menopausal women get hot flashes. They are intensified by stress and sometimes are accompanied by night sweats.[16] Some scarely notice them. Others are drenched with sweat and turn deeply red.

In *Hot Flashes,* Barbara Raskin describes how hot flashes feel and the insights one can get from them:

> Totally absorbed in some intellectual problem, I will suddenly feel like I've just opened an oven door to lift the lid off a turkey roaster, allowing a stream of steam to escape and slap my face.[17]
>
> More and more frequently nowadays, my hot flashes have begun to feel like urgent communiques from the interior of a vast, dark continent—fast-breaking news items from my heart of darkness. Sometimes hot flashes trigger sudden insights into previously obscure experiences. Other times, in reverse fashion, a rush of revelations will release the heat like thunder after a flash of lightning. Either way, I have come to trust the wired insights that hot flashes produce.[18]
>
> Because I believe in epiphanies, I record most of these illuminations in a notebook that I carry in my purse. Since hot flashes are often cryptic, I try to decipher their meanings as soon as possible.[19]

Although the level of estrogen declines at menopause, sex drive does not necessarily decrease. In fact, many women report an increased interest in and desire for sex.[20]

Middle-aged women, however, often find themselves sexually out of sync with middle-aged men who may be losing their sexual vigor, and although our culture condones the older man-younger woman couple, it looks down on the older woman-younger man pair.

Depression is a "symptom" which affects some menopausal women in this culture. Phyllis Chesler thinks that it is not surprising that older women get depressed, because "...their already limited opportunities for sexual, emotional, and intellectual growth decrease even further."[21]

It is questionable whether the negative associations with mid-life—depression, irritability, anxiety, and sadness—are really "menopausal," or reasonable reactions to what is currently happening in the woman's life. Are these reactions indicative of the way a menopausal woman is diminished in youth-glorifying America?

> A cumulative effect develops and, one day, you yell out, "*Enough!*" That is called a menopausal outburst. It can be for any reason. Enough times making the dinner, enough times cleaning up after people, enough times going to the supermarket. Enough of the countless, repetitious, unthanked jobs, done without joy, often without acknowledgment, let alone reward.[22]

Menopause is also a sign of aging, and with all our emphasis on youth, it is sometimes difficult for middle-aged women to see themselves as beautiful. Thus, menopause is indeed a depressing time for women who fear the loss of their youth.

Osteoporosis, the condition of porous or fragile bones, is associated with aging, and can become more severe with increased age. However, that it is directly caused by menopause and the subsequent drop in estrogen, or that it is a natural part of aging is controversial. In a forthcoming book on osteoporosis from an anthropological perspective, Susan E. Brown shows that osteoporosis is not uniformly distributed among all aged persons in all cultures. In fact, some aged people never suffer from bone loss, and rates of bone loss vary from culture to culture.[23]

In some parts of the world, men have a higher incidence of osteoporosis, including hip fracutures, than women. Rib and sternum fractures occur with much greater frequency throughout the world among elderly males than females.[24]

Low-technology, traditional cultures appear to have the lowest incidence of osteoporosis. Brown theorizes that industrialized countries have a high rate of osteoporosis among women because women spend more time inside under artificial lights than men and don't get enough exposure to sunlight and therefore vitamin D; women do less physical exercise; women use more prescription drugs and have more medical intervention than men; women often have their ovaries removed and men rarely their testicles; many women have a poor diet with inadequate calcium in their efforts to keep thin (85% of adolescent and adult females don't get adequate calcium).[25]

Documented risk factors for osteoporosis are: smoking, alcoholism, lack of exercise, ovary removal, use of steroids and certain other medications (antacids containing aluminum, excessive thyroxine, various anticonvulsant drugs), family history, slight build and small stature, increased age, being female and Caucasian, vitamin D deficiency, and high fat and protein intake. A high protein intake is detrimental to one's calcium balance, as is a high salt intake.[26]

Weight gain is another concern at menopause. A desire to eat more can have many emotional causes, but Reitz suggests that women at menopause may have an increased appetite caused by the chemical changes in their bodies, and that women should be aware of this and not fight it, it will settle down.[27] Exercise is vital, however, to balance this tendency.

"Thinner walls" in the vagina, which predispose some women to pain during intercourse and more frequent infections, is often mentioned as a symptom of menopause. Vaginal dryness is another symptom. But, says Reitz, "...regular sex, which includes masturbation, makes these changes hardly noticeable."[28] She stresses that these changes are not negative, but merely different from a younger woman's vagina. Older women's bodies are not "abnormal" simply by virtue of being different from younger women's bodies.

What to Do

Recommendations for making menopause easier are: get plenty of rest, respect the changes your body is going through, take care of your skin with rubs and oils, eat sensibly, and "value yourself as important, even though the culture doesn't."[29]

Reitz suggests keeping a journal of feelings and emotions, as well as a record of periods: dates, type of flow, length of symptoms.[30] Keeping a journal is helpful because it makes us more aware of what is happening.

The first thing doctors are likely to recommend for menopausal symptoms is tranquilizers. Reitz says these "...are especially important in keeping menopausal women quiet and out of sight... Do you know what would happen if all the women between 40 and 55 started making demands? My adrenaline begins to burst forth at the excitement of the idea."[31]

Although many women feel anxious, and for good reason (including jobs, mates, what we haven't done, what we're going to do), tranquilizers are rarely the solution. Tranquilizers are often more for the benefit of others; they are addictive and they eradicate necessary REM sleep. Women should not deny their feelings. They should let out their anger.

For hot flashes, Reitz advises dressing in layers. Take off the outer clothing when a hot flash occurs, she says, and breathe deeply. She urges women to tell family, friends, and co-workers what is happening, instead of hiding hot flashes out of shame.[32]

Some women take estrogen for hot flashes, but there are side effects, including a relationship between estrogen and cancer which is lessened by adding progesterone.[33] However, progesterone has its own effect upon the body and no one knows the end results of its long-term use. Also, hot flashes recur if estrogen therapy is stopped.

> Our bodies are not suddenly deprived of estrogen as some would have us believe. Rather, the lesser amount produced by the ovaries is the natural, normal way for our bodies to function at an age when we are no longer desirous of bearing children. To change that by supplying estrogen from the outside is to disrupt our natural process, for all the endocrine glands in the body are interrelated. The healthy functioning of one depends on all the others.[34]

Are women being sold a cure they don't need, and worse, a cure that is dangerous? The risk of breast and uterine cancer clearly rises with the use of estrogen. Men who take estrogen for prostate cancer have developed cancer of the breast.[35]

It is estimated that 25 million prescriptions a year are written in the U.S. for estrogen replacement drugs. The boom in estrogen consumption came about with a three-fold message to women in the 1960s: Dr. Robert Wilson's *Feminine Forever,* which advocated estrogen replacement therapy; articles in women's magazines; and propaganda, in the form of ads, booklets, and messages to doctors, by Ayerst Laboratories which manufactures estrogen. The FDA has discredited Robert Wilson, who was subsidized by Ayerst and who suggested that women start taking estrogen in their thirties and continue with it for the rest of their lives, calling him an "unacceptable investigator."[36]

Estrogen is still highly touted as the preferred treatment for preventing bone loss in post-menopausal women.[37] However, not only is its safety questionable, but according to Brown who studied osteoporosis cross-culturally, so is its effectiveness. If osteoporosis were caused by a lack of estrogen, osteoporosis would be a universal phenomenon. Brown has found that osteoporosis is non-existent among the elderly in some cultures, and in many its incidence is far below that of the U.S. and other industrialized countries. Also, there is evidence that osteoporosis can start before menopause when estrogen is still being produced in high quantities.[38]

Treatment for osteoporosis is highly controversial. Even the importance of calcium is unclear, as most of the world has a lower calcium intake than the U.S. *and* lower osteoporosis rates. Incidence of osteoporosis seems to also depend on intake of protein, amount of exercise, and exposure to sunlight.[39]

LAST QUARTER

Doris Henderson

The moon is full tonight;
once in every twenty-eight days,
thirteen times a year,
my blood moves to her cycles...
thirteen months in the ancient calendar,
reign of the Goddess:
Luna inlustris in singulos menses;
luna in sanguine nostra...

He shook my hand, nice gesture,
pretending we were equals in this game;
but he held all the weapons:
in the examining room, my heels stuck firmly in the
stirrups,
rubber gloves, metal instrument probing my depths...
I gripped the table top,

told him yes or no it didn't hurt;
hard fingers poked my belly while the other hand
claimed all my inner space.

When it was over I sat jelly-bottomed in my paper gown,
greased inside like a roasting hen.
My cold feet dangled from the table in the antiseptic air...
"You may get dressed now."

Behind the big desk he was more talkative;
clipped Indian accent, British taught:
"Not an emergency, but it should come out.
At your age, it is no longer functional.
New technique—no abdominal cuts—all done from
  underneath,
like pulling out the giblets on Thanksgiving eve,
leaving a nice, clean, empty space—
"The o-var-eez, we will take them too;
soon they will not be functional;
they could become cancerous."
(So could your liver, Doctor.)

  My blood comes more slowly now,
  sometimes forgets—
  these little clocks, oval witches, o-var-eez,
  dropping their magic potions
  to the cycle of the moon;
  breasts and belly softer as
  the clocks run down, but gently, in their own time—

Your knife is sharp and ready;
you will have me sense-dead, shaven
under your thousand-watt bulbs,
draw out my womb, extract it living
like an old fat slippery frog.
White-gowned surgeon, flanked by admiring aides,
you will not remember that you grew inside a frog
  identical...

In days to come I will sit
listless in your waiting room;
injections timed by your appointment book,
giving me back those potions
bottled, measured, priced at the current rate...

Tonight there is yet time-
I drive home in the gathering night,
roofs and hedgerows tipped in silver
under the lustrous moon—

Little clocks,
held by small tendrils,
wise women,
sending their magic fluids
to the rhythms of the moon:
leading me gently, slowly, softly,
into old age...

Other Cultures

In some North and South American Indian cultures, postmenopausal women are no longer thought to be polluting, and it is a time when "many women acquire a special status in the community, taking on ceremonial roles such as supervisor of menarcheal ceremonies; becoming midwives, herbalists, or shamans." Before menopause, these women were not allowed to participate alongside men in religious and political activities.[40]

Marcha Flint studied menopausal women in other cultures and found that where there was a valuable role for women to assume, there did not seem to be problems associated with menopause other than some physiological ones, "no depressions, dizziness, no incapacitations." Women who were considered "unclean" while menstruating were now able to join together with men and were worthy of respect and "even veneration."[41]

Concurring with these studies, Pauline Bart found that in all the cultures she studied, the role a woman played in her fertile years was reversed at menopause.[42]

Another cross-cultural study found that hot flashes were the one menopausal symptom that existed in all the cultures studied, suggesting that this symptom is physiologically related to menopause. Depression was not found to be directly related to menopause.[43]

Osteoporosis is also not a necessary component of menopause, according to Susan Brown's cross-cultural anthropological perspective. Some cultures do not exhibit osteoporosis at all in post-menopausal women, and in others, osteoporosis has been found in men and pre-menopausal women.[44] (See discussion under "What Happens at Menopause.")

In present-day Japan, attitudes toward menopause seem considerably different from those in the U.S. From data collected in the early 1980s in Tokyo and in the countryside, by interviewing women aged 35 to 60, these results were obtained: more than half believed that menopause was the best time of a woman's life, because of free time and energy available; only approximately 15% believed that women lose their "feminine attractiveness" at menopause and that menopausal women should not be given important work to do.[45]

In Japan, many women believe that acupuncture and herbal medicines can make these natural processes more comfortable. All symptoms, physical and psychological, are treated without differentiation and with no labels given. The body is put in balance, and no hormones or tranquilizers are used.[46]

In other times, other societies, older women were sought out for their wisdom:

> The rites were often governed by old women, due to the ancient belief that post-menopausal women were the wisest of mortals because they permanently retained their "wise blood." In the 17th century A.D., Christian writers still insisted that old women were filled with magic power because their menstrual blood remained in their veins. This was the real reason why old women were constantly persecuted for witchcraft. The same "magic blood" that made them leaders in the ancient clan system made them objects of fear under the new patriarchal faith.[47]

The following is an example of how these wise women are honored in a present-day society.

GRANDMOTHER LODGE

Brooke Medicine Eagle

The Grandmother Lodge is the lodge of the white-haired (wisdom) women—those who have gone beyond the time of giving away the power of their blood, and now hold it for energy to uphold the Law.

When our elders step across the threshold of the Grandmother Lodge, leaving their bleeding behind them, they become the Keepers of the Law. No longer is their attention consumed with the creation and rearing of their own family. In this sense, they have no children, and in our ways those who are not parent to any specific child are parent to ALL CHILDREN. Thus their attention turns to the children of All Our Relations: not just their own children, or the children of their friends, their clan or tribe, but the children of all the hoops: the Two-Leggeds, the Four-Leggeds, the Wingeds, the Finned, the Green-Growing Ones, and all others. Our relationship with this great circle of Life rests ultimately in their hands. They must give-away this responsibility by modeling, teaching, and sharing the living of this law in everyday life—to men, women, children—that all might come into balance.

What this means for women, in very practical terms, is this. When you pass beyond menopause, you have the opportunity for a renewed and deeply powerful experience of yourself. As you drop away from the silliness and fear that has been generated by the "over the hill" cultural trance, and open yourself to the truth that lives within you—body and spirit—you will find an incredible challenge—a challenge for which you are better equipped than any other two-legged. You have the opportunity to sit in council, and using the power of the blood held among you, create a harmonious world around you.

Let me speak for a moment of women's moon-time (menstrual) blood and its power. This blood has been shown to be among the (if not THE) most nurturing, bio-energizing substance on Earth. When placed upon plants, they are deeply nourished. In our native ways, during our ceremonies of planting and nurturing our crops, we had moon-time women (women in the days of their menses) move among the plants and give-away their blood. Always, our women gave-away this wonderful blood in an honoring way. They sat upon the ground and gave-away directly, or bled upon moss and later placed it upon the Earth to nurture and renew. Vicki Noble reminds us that this blood was the first blood offered on the altar—a most blessed gift. Then when women were no longer honored and the power of their life-giving blood was ignored, animal and human sacrifice was used to give blood on the altar.

This is the blood, then, that you hold among you when you no longer bleed in the moon-cycle; you have passed your moontime. Elders, perhaps you have not been aware of the profound responsibility you are now to assume: if you had known you would have had the conscious opportunity to learn and deepen yourself in good relationship through your lifetime, so that you might serve your people and use yourself well in these years. Younger women, you who read this now are conscious and can choose to learn and grow in this way, that you might feel ready when you, too, step into the Grandmother Lodge.

Among many of the tribes the primacy of the Law of Good Relationship was remembered and the Grandmother Lodges, or the societies within it, were known to hold the highest command. If a peace chief was not leading his people across the land in a way that all people and animals had good food, clear water, and sheltering valleys in the time of cold winds, then the Grandmothers asked for someone new to lead; they called someone to step forth for the people who had the probability of doing a better job in his active work to nurture and renew the people. If a war chief was creating such animosity among surrounding tribes that frequent attacks disrupted the life and well-being of the people, he was asked to find productive rather than destructive uses for his energy. Such was the power of the Grandmothers: they took seriously the charge to nurture and renew the people, and took action in line with it.

The Grandmother Lodge was the lodge of all post-menopausal women. Within that, smaller groups formed around their various functions. For some women, it might be the keeping of a sacred basket, for others a certain kind of healing, and for yet others the maintaining of a beauty way (art) among the people. A basket weaver might belong to a basket-makers' society and also to a society that maintained a sacred bundle (these latter often came through family lineages). A woman might belong to a ceremonial Sun Dance society, and as well to a society of herbalists.

As you begin gathering with others now, you will likely have a small and mixed group, and need to determine the common interests, skills, and goals among you. Perhaps you will choose a focus of 1) speaking to children's classes about the

Grandmother Lodge; 2) working with the Rainforest Action Group; 3) creating a babysitting service for working mothers; or 4) speaking to men's groups on issues of harmony and good relationship—the possibilities for good are endless. Some of your time together may well be to increase your own learning and understanding—meetings to share skills with each other, to meditate and learn to listen to the Great Voices Within, gatherings to hike upon the Earth or to strengthen and tone your bodies.

Something I am often asked is about those of you who have experienced amenorrhea, early menopause, or hysterectomies. Where do you fit? Although I cannot say I know the exact answers, this is what makes sense to me through my own experience. The first thought I have is that you will very likely want to get a sense of the rhythm of activity/receptivity—worldly action/great Mystery—that is your natural cycle in synchrony with Grandmother Moon for this cycle still echoes through the waters of your body even though external bleeding does not accompany it. Deepen your experience of the moon's cycle within you, it is very powerful and useful for you and All Your Relations to reach through the veil into the Great Mystery during your bleeding and bring back vision for your people. Secondly, many of us who are younger and don't yet experience ourselves as elders are being called into the Grandmother Lodge because there is an urgent need for the awakening of this function among women. Because of the crushing of the native cultures and the loss of the women's ways, there are few who sit in these Lodges and uphold the nurturing and renewing of the people. So younger, awakened ones of us are being called into the Lodge through many different means. Accept it as an honor.

The final aspect of the Grandmother Lodge I will address is the rite of passage into it. Those of you surrounding a woman who is crossing this threshold will want to honor this special woman and to let her know of your support of her in this time of her great responsibility. There are many ways this can be done and I will suggest only a few: ritual bathing and anointing by her closest friend, then being dressed in a white gown (for wisdom) and a red sash (to represent the blood, or life force, in All Our Relations and the dedication to them) for a circle dance and feasting; an honoring of her by each woman gathered expressing her appreciation for this woman; a special dedication from the honored one can be given. Certainly an invocation of the Goddess, of White Buffalo Woman or the Wise Crone can be done—perhaps in the form of a guided meditation for the elder one to deepen her contact with this source of strength and wisdom. You who know her will know those aspects which have special meaning for her. Always when I do such a ritual, I include as part of the rite, the charging of this woman with the primary responsibility of the nurturing and renewing of All Her Relations—and remind her of Creator's Law of Good Relationship. Among you, one already in her Grandmother Lodge might perform this function.

BLOOD LOOSENS ITS STRANGLE-HOLD

Margaret Randall

Why is not how...
it is meaning...
—Susan Sherman

My age moves its monthly burden of blood
as opening a book to a particular page, hot and why,
our hands stay where they will
my body stays where it will, waiting.
Blood loosens its strangle-hold upon my running feet.

We chose to ignore the writing *and* the wall, the dream
filled our eyes, we didn't want
the commercials.
Somewhere a bell ringing through motionless air
announced a separation of sisters.

We understood that why is not how
beyond words, with a great voice we knew
there is power called creativity
wearing a mask called change.
I know because you taught me this.

All these years beyond placebos filling our mouths,
slivers
of glass and sand tearing our feet
we knew beyond mixed messages and no message
beyond heavy rules and door closed
by others and also by ourselves.

The face that said no the arms that said no the grace
of god or patriarch.
We understood and the Island dried our tears.
We stood our ground.
We stand our ground.

SOMETHING TO LOOK FORWARD TO

Marge Piercy

Menopause—word used as an insult:
a menopausal woman, mind or poem
as if not to leak regularly or on the caprice
of the moon, the collision of egg and sperm,
were the curse we first learned to call that blood.

I have twisted myself to praise that bright splash.
When my womb opens its lips on the full
or dark of the moon, that connection
aligns me as it does the sea. I quiver,
a compass needle thrilling with magnetism.

Yet for every celebration there's the time
it starts on a jet with the seatbelt sign on.
Consider the trail of red amoebae
crawling onto hostess's sheets to signal
my body's disregard of calendar, clock.

How often halfway up the side of a mountain,
during a demonstration with the tactical police
force drawn up in tanks between me and a toilet;
during an endless wind machine panel with four males
I the token woman and they with iron bladders,

I have felt that wetness and wanted to strangle
my womb like a mouse. Sometimes it feels cosmic
and sometimes it feels like mud. Yes, I have prayed
to my blood on my knees in toilet stalls
simply to show its rainbow of deliverance.

My friend Penny at twelve, being handed a napkin
the size of an ironing board cover, cried out
Do I have to do this from now till I die?
No, said her mother, it stops in middle age.
Good, said Penny, there's something to look forward to.

Today supine, groaning with demon crab claws
gouging my belly, I tell you I will secretly dance
and pour out a cup of wine on the earth
when time stops that leak permanently;
I will burn my last tampons as votive candles.

Women responding to the questionnaire wrote of their thoughts about menopause:

— I've thought that I would like to have a ritual for myself to celebrate keeping my blood in myself.

— I am ambivalent. Look forward to no more bloody sheets but will miss this week I take each month to care for my own needs as opposed to my husband's.

— Curiosity; feel I'll have a graceful process. Some negativity, opposite of the traditional kind, because I'll miss menstruating.

— Mostly negative as our male models view this and expectations portrayed are negative, i.e., it means I am old, barren, etc. I am sure when the time comes I'll develop my own meaning and joy around it.

Our society does not honor the passage we make from being fertile to non-fertile; and because of this, as with menarche, women must honor themselves and devise their own ceremonies. One woman writes:

> My dream is to develop my own rite of passage, invite those to attend who are special to me, sacrifice some symbol of that which is past, pay homage to the wisdom within which is the product of my years on this planet, and celebrate with food, drink, and music. There are gifts to being older, and we each need to recognize them. Women are fortunate in that they have a definite event that marks the passage into the time of wisdom.[48]

Menopause is a time for re-evaluation. For those women who were responsible for raising children, that phase of life is probably ending. Women will likely have more time for themselves, and can use this as an opportuity to follow paths previously untaken.

A third of a woman's life, or more, comes after menopause, and these years can be vital, zestful, creative, to be spent in pursuing personal and social dreams. They can also be sexy years.

> To be free of the worry of having a tampon or sanitary napkin at hand...To be free from staining underwear and cramps...To be liberated from conception; not to worry about birth control; to be able, at any time one feels like it...to be sexual, with no concern or preparations. To enter upon a new cycle of life, while one is still vigorous, and yet have the benefit of experience, and for many women, to confront death, to realize time is limited and to value it to the point of allowing no room for deception. These are positive feelings about menopause.[49]

Epilogue

DARDENELLA

Dorothy Rose

I can forget about diaphragms, modess, and tampons. Hallelujah! I can jump into bed with complete abandon. My periodic flow has ceased. My womb sheds no more tears. The end brings back memories of the beginnings.

Where is Dardenella now, my childhood informant. The one who told me that there was no Santa Claus, that there was probably no God, and that that Jesus stuff was just a bunch of crap that grown-ups used to keep kids in line, to keep you from having fun. She taught me how to masturbate with her under the cover when we played house, always making me be the Daddy. Of course, I never touched her body. It was always my finger on her panties, and Jimmie was our baby. He was too young for anything else. And never mind that she didn't have the information right about sex or a lot of other things. I liked her explanations and her daring. I would have followed her into the fire before I would have believed or listened to anyone else, especially the Sunday school teacher. Dardenella said nothing was really a sin, but just to be sure, never tell anyone what she told me or what we did. As soon as she found out anything that was a sin, she'd tell me what it was, and we would do it. And another thing she said was, always remember to wash your hands with soap and water, and put some Jergens lotion on them, just in case your mother asks to smell them.

She said that when you get your period, you get it just once. Then you are through with that, and after that you could get pregnant and have a baby, even if you only held hands with a boy, providing he used his middle finger to scratch your palm, especially if you both are sweating. So that's one thing you have to be careful about.

When she found out that your period comes every month, she came to me with the new information. She said to forget about that holding hand stuff. It's kissing that does it. Especially if he puts his tongue in your mouth when you are on your period. That's why some people call it the "curse."

Then the day after she had read one of her brother's True Story magazines that she found under his mattress, she decided it happens if a boy touches your breast when you are not on your period. Why would he want to do a silly thing like that, I asked her, and she said boys are bad, just full of sin, and that they don't have to worry because they can never get pregnant. And she said if they suck both of your breasts, that you would have twins.

After that we were so busy sneaking into picture shows on Sunday afternoons, and thinking of going to dances on Saturday nights, and reading Modern Romances, and painting our lips and fingernails bright red, and telling lies to our parents and Sunday school teachers, and every other sin that we knew how to do, that by the time we had our first real date, she floored me with the newest information. THE REAL McCOY. To get pregnant, a girl and boy had to do what we had seen Queenie and Spot do. And she didn't know if it was when you were on your period or when you were not on your period for sure.

We were really astounded with this new idea. We looked at each other. Gosh, that could mean that our parents had done it five times each. This we couldn't fathom. But we were sure that Randolph Richet's mamma and daddy had done that awful thing. They had ten kids, and everybody knew that they were trash.

We had been reading a lot of books, and it seemed that the girl "did it" a lot of times, and for some reason she did not get pregnant ever. But then we had seen a lot of Westerns and men were shooting a lot of other men, and they were lying dead all over the place, and no one ever stopped to bury them. There was never a funeral. It was kind of like "doing it"; nothing much happened afterwards, maybe. Dardenella had overheard her mother telling someone that to keep from getting pregnant you're supposed to cross something—your eyes, your self, or was it your fingers? Just what it was, she couldn't remember.

Before I got married, because I didn't understand my body, I was swallowed by fear and ignorance, and that lightning bolt of sex created a guilt that hung in the air like thunder. I was not afraid of VD nor was I afraid that God would strike me down if I "did it." I had the fear of one thing, and one thing alone. Pregnancy. If I "did it" and got pregnant, that would be worse than dying or getting cancer. I would have to do something about it. Fast. I couldn't just stand there. I would have to get married, jump from the Golden Gate Bridge, get an abortion, or have the baby.

I had visions of walking down the aisle. The wedding march is playing. There is a big red spot on the back of my gown, and blood is running down my legs, splashing on the white carpet. Or I am walking down the aisle, my belly is sticking out nine months. There is no blood. But everyone is running out of the church, even the minister. Or I sit on the edge of the pool, dangling my feet. Some boy pushes me into the water, and a red river gushes forth around me.

After marriage, from month to month, with a mixture of fear and dread combined, I awaited the coming of my period as if its failure would be earth-shaking. Every night for three weeks out of the month, I went to bed when my husband went to bed. On the fourth week I could stay up late to paint, to read, to think and to write. With each pregnancy, the blood stopped while my body expanded, gorged with life. Then it was split, emptied, and drained with the bloody ritual of childbearing.

Life suddenly grows dark. I feel depressed because I have reached a point in life when I realize I am not and can never hope to be the person I once believed I would become. I feel guilty because I have lived this long, and I want to live longer. I am still chasing the hummingbird. It is said that if you catch one you will live to be 100. I feel crushed under this change. Thoughts of sex, the oldest of things, spring forth once again. I ask the question, is sex everything or is everything sex? Is the whole world just one big fuck?

I know that this is the beginning of the end. But so is birth. The mystery of life cannot be solved. It can only be lived through. I hope that the beauty of age goes to the bone. I look inward as I take a forward step into the rhythm of life. I continue the process of forever becoming.

Dardenella, as you hold this page at arm's length in order to clear the print, I hope your hot flashes are cool ones.

Women are rhythmical beings, following the moon's cycle of waxing and waning. Ovulating and bleeding. We have an opportunity every month to 'descend,' like Persephone, into the underworld, the underworld being our self, our soul, our deepest being. And from these depths we can emerge with knowledge, insight, new creations.

Menstruation is a time for sleeping and dreaming, meditation, yoga, and dancing. A time for healing, being creative, figuring things out. A dark and inward time, a sensual time, a powerful time.

And yet, it is precisely this phase of our cycle—the pre-menstrual days and the bleeding itself—that we are taught to ignore, to be ashamed of, even to despise. What a terrible loss for Woman. And more, what a terrible loss for all the world.

> If you have ever lived with the seasons of the East, you know the joy of cyclic change. So too, with menstruation. Only after menopause do you realize how tangible the periods were as to feminity and the cleansing feeling accompanying the periods. You were in touch with the moon.[1]

> ...We know the balancing of life and death, growing and letting go. Bleeding teaches us gentleness. How being slow and delicate in movement stills the mind.[2]

In writing this book I have talked to a great many women (and men) on every aspect of menstruation, and their comments have shaped my own thinking. I am still learning, and would like to hear from you regarding your own experiences and your reactions to this book. Thank you.

Appendix I

Menstruation Questionnaire

I am doing research on how women feel about menstruation, and eventually plan to publish a book on the subject. Some of the information received from these questionnaires may be included in the book. I may also want to use some direct quotes; if this is all right with you, please sign, date and put your address in the space provided at the end. I am very grateful to the women who take the time to answer these questions. I feel that menstruation is an important aspect of women's lives, and one on which little research has been done. If you have reached menopause, answer the questions as they applied to you when menstruating. If you need more space for responses, use extra paper and indicate which question number you are writing about. Thank you!

Age______________ Age at menarche (first period) ______________

1. Who "prepared" you for menstruation (mother, sister, friend, church, school, nobody)?
2. How did they do it?
3. What kind of experience was your menarche for you?
4. Did you have any inkling before you started that it was about to happen, e.g., bodily sensations, dreams, etc.?
5. If you have any problems associated with your periods, what are they and what do you do about them?
6. Do you "celebrate" menstruation in any way by doing something special at that time?
7. What is the funniest thing that ever happened to you regarding your periods?
8. Are your dreams different around the time you are menstruating? If so, how?
9. Are your sexual feelings and experiences in any way different around the time of your period? If so, how?
10. How would you describe your energy level during menstruation?
11. What do you most like to do while you are menstruating?
12. Are there any traditions in your family or culture which you observe concerning menstruation?
13. What do you use to absorb your menstrual blood?
14. If there are other women who menstruate in your household, do you menstruate at about the same time?
15. Have you noticed things that affect the way you feel around the time of your period, such as diet, coffee, herbs, stress, exercise, etc.? And *how* do these things affect you?
16. In what ways does menstruation *enrich* your life, if any?
17. Is there anything else you'd like to say about how you feel about menstruation?
18. What are your thoughts about menopause?

The purpose of this questionnaire was to find out, in women's own words, their attitudes and feelings about menstruation. It was not meant to be a scientific study with a random sample; rather, it was a survey of menstrual practices, attitudes, and emotional and physical feelings. The questionnaire was given to friends, distributed in women's studies classes, and sent to some of the women who responded to my calls for material. A total of fifty-three were completed and returned.

Thirty-eight percent of the respondents were from California, followed by 19% from New York, 9% from Massachusetts, 8% from Oregon, and the rest scattered throughout the U.S. The age range was from 19 to 65, with 53% being between the ages of 32 and 41.

Sixty-eight percent of the women were taught about menstruation by their mothers, 17% from school instruction (some received information from both mother and school), and 10% said no one prepared them. For the majority of respondents, menarche was a negative experience, with 62% saying it was scary, painful, embarrassing, confusing, lonely, or they were not prepared. Twenty-five percent said their menarche was exciting and they were glad they started. Six percent said it was "nothing much."

Although nearly two-thirds of the women said they did not have any inkling that their periods were about to start for the first time, over 25% did have some idea. Most of these "felt different." ("As I remember it I suddenly felt utterly different, as if I was in the grip of something enormous and would never be the same again.") Some had cramps; one had a dream and another a "tickling sensation."

Sixty-four percent of the respondents said they experienced some kind of discomfort during menstruation, either PMS or cramps. A small number also mentioned constipation, bloating, and breast pain. The women listed the following as remedies: aspirin or other medication; vitamins; calcium; herbs; rest or sleep; orgasms; meditation and acupuncture; cutting out caffeine, sugar and salt.

Forty-two percent of the women said they do not celebrate menstruation except perhaps the fact that they are not pregnant. Nearly a third, however, celebrate by doing something special (going out, lighting red candles, being alone) or pampering themselves (buying treats, having long baths).

Few women could think of anything funny. One woman wrote that the funniest thing was filling out this questionnaire. Another said she is only 20 years old, so she has "twenty more years to be really amused." The funny accounts were probably embarrassing as much as funny, e.g., "One Sunday I went to my mother-in-law's with the children and my husband for dinner. Relaxed and seated we stayed and talked and I, with my period, had soaked through the chair. My husband, quick-thinking, removed all the dishes from my mother-in-law's table and wrapped the tablecloth around me."

Fifty-three percent said their dreams were no different around the time of menstruation, and 43% said they were, most of these saying they were more sexual and more vivid.

However, 85% said their sexual feelings and experiences were different at this time, and of these, 78% said that just before or during menstruation they felt more sexual, or that their sexual feelings were more intense. ("When I start feeling real gut-level desire I know I'm about to bleed.")

On the question of energy level, 55% of the women said their energy was low during menstruation, particularly at the beginning. Fifteen percent said their energy level was up-and-down, and 13% described theirs as "high."

Nearly everyone listed a quiet, relaxing activity as what they like to do during menstruation, e.g., read, stay in bed, be alone, sleep, paint, write, garden, take it easy, meditate, take baths.

Only 13% said there were menstruation traditions in their family or culture. These were given as the Jewish spank at menarche; keeping separate from men; not swimming; meeting with other menstruating women; and a ritual bath. One woman wrote: "My mother thought she was doing a good thing by passing on the tradition of slapping my cheeks to 'keep the blush' in them when I told her about the blood stains on my panties. I interpreted her slap as punishment and felt I must have done something wrong, even though she explained the meaning behind the slap when she saw the tears in my eyes."

As for absorbing the menstrual blood, 66% of the women said they use tampons, and 51% said they use pads. (Some respondents used more than one type of product.) Nine percent each used sponges and rags, two women made their own pads, and one used nothing.

Sixty percent of the women said they did menstruate in synchronicity with other women they lived or worked with. (One woman works with ten other women and they all menstruate about the same time.) In fact, only 4% said they did not. The remaining respondents said this question was not applicable.

On the question of what affects how women feel while they are menstruating, 30% said stress makes them feel worse, and 25% said caffeine does. Others said sugar affects them adversely. Thirty-four percent said exercise helps them to counteract these effects, and several women listed a healthy diet (whole grain, low sugar and salt), herb teas and other liquids as helpful. Some women wrote that they crave sugar, coffee, spicy foods, and food in general, but these do not necessarily make them feel good.

Seventy-nine percent of the women said menstruation does enrich their life in some way, usually by putting them in touch with their body, their femaleness, the cyclicity of life, reminding them of what is important. Only 9% said it did not enrich their lives.

As for thoughts on menopause, 32% of the women had generally positive attitudes toward it, another 11% said they were looking forward to it (in some cases, because it would be an end to menstruation), 21% said they were worried or anxious about menopause, and 11% had mixed feelings.

Appendix II

Resources and Readings

Bart, Pauline, "Menopause," *Women and Health,* May/June, 1976, pp. 3-11.

Berry, Carolyn, "Celebrating the Blood: Indian Women and Menstruation," *Bread & Roses,* Vol. 3, No. 2, 1984.

Boston Women's Health Book Collective, *The New Our Bodies, Ourselves*. New York: Simon & Schuster, 1984.

Brown, Susan E., *Osteoporosis in Anthropological Perspective,* a forthcoming book. For information contact The Nutrition Education and Consulting Service, 1200 E. Genesee St., Suite 310, Syracuse, New York 13210. Points the way to a revision of commonly accepted assumptions about osteoporosis.

Buckley, Thomas, "Menstruation and the power of Yurok women: methods of cultural reconstruction," *American Ethnologist,* 9, pp. 47-60.

Chesler, Phyllis, *About Men*. New York: Bantam Books, 1978.

Delaney, Janice, Mary Jane Lupton, and Emily Toth, *The Curse*. New York: E.P. Dutton & Co., Inc., 1976.

Doress, Paula Brown and Diana Laskin Siegal, *Ourselves, Growing Older*. New York: Simon & Schuster, 1987.

Dudley, Rosemary J., "She Who Bleeds, Yet Does Not Die," in *Heresies,* No. 5, pp. 112-116.

Edelson, Mary Beth, "Menstruation Stories"

Farrer, Claire, "Singing for Life: The Mescalero Apache Girls' Puberty Ceremony," *Betwixt & Between: Patterns of Masculine and Feminine Initiation,* ed. Louise Mahdi, Steven Foster and Meredith Little. La Salle, IL: Open Court, 1987.

Flint, Marcha, "The Menopause: Reward or Punishment?" in *Psychosomatics,* Vol. 16, pp. 161-3, Fourth Quarter 1975.

Flowers, Felicity Artemis, *The P.M.S. Conspiracy,* Circle of Aradia Publications, 4111 Lincoln Blvd #211, Marina del Rey, CA 90292. Copies may be ordered from this address. Feminist view of PMS.

Ford, Lynda Ross, *Bleeding—A Celebration*. Albion, CA: Aguila Press, 1983.

Friedman, Nancy, *Everything You Must Know About Tampons*. New York: Berkley Books, 1981.
Grahn, Judy, "From Sacred Blood to the Curse and Beyond," *The Politics of Women's Spirituality,* ed. Charlene Spretnak. New York: Anchor Press, 1982.
Harding, Esther, *Woman's Mysteries*. New York: Harper Colophon Books, 1971.
Knight, Chris, "Levi-Strauss and the Dragon: Mythologiques Reconsidered in the Light of an Australian Aboriginal Myth," *Man,* Vol. 18, 1983, pp. 21-50.
Laws, Sophie, Valerie Hey and Andrea Eagan, *Seeing Red*. London: Hutchinson & Co. Ltd, 1985. This book does not "deny physical difference nor dismiss the effects of cyclical changes in women's bodies." Instead, it raises questions about how these are perceived within a patriarchal society.
Leavitt, Ruby Rohrlich, *Peaceable Primates and Gentle People: Anthropological Approaches to Women's Studies*. New York: Harper & Row, Inc., 1975.
Lincoln, Bruce, *Emerging from the Chrysalis*. Cambridge, MA: Harvard University Press, 1981.
Mankowitz, Ann, *Change of Life—A Psychological Study of Dreams and the Menopause*. Toronto, Canada: Inner City Books, 1984.
Medicine Eagle, Brooke, "Women's Moontime—A Call to Power," *Shaman's Drum,* Spring 1986.
Modesto, Ruby and Guy Mount, *Not for Innocent Ears*. Arcata, CA: Sweetlight Books, 1980.
Nagy, Marilyn, "Menstruation and Shamanism," *Betwixt & Between: Patterns of Masculine and Feminine Initiation,* Ed. Louise Mahdi, Steven Foster and Meredith Little. La Salle, IL: Open Court Publishers, 1987.
Noble, Vicki, "Female Blood--Roots of Shamanism," *Shaman's Drum,* Spring 1986.
Notelovitz, Morris and Marsha Ware, *Stand Tall*. New York: Bantam Books, 1985.
Olesen, Virginia and Nancy Fugate Woods, eds., *Culture, Society, and Menstruation*. Washington: Hemisphere Publishing Corp., 1986.
"On Becoming A Woman: Mothers and Daughters Talking Together," a film from the National Black Women's Health Project, Directed by Cheryl Chisholm. Includes a wonderful discussion between mothers and daughters about their first menstrual periods. For more information, contact the National Black Women's Health Project, 1236 Gordon St. S.W., Atlanta, GA 30310.
Parvati, Jeannine, *Hygieia*. Monroe, Utah: Freestone Publishing Co., 1978. Includes a comprehensive discussion on the use of herbs to alleviate menstrual discomfort and for regulating menstrual flow.

Powers, Marla N., "Menstruation and Reproduction: An Oglala Case," in *Women—Sex & Sexuality,* ed. Catherine Stimson and Ethel Person. Chicago: University of Chicago Press, 1981.

Reitz, Rosetta, *Menopause—A Positive Approach.* New York: Penguin Books, 1977. Reitz says, "My hope for this book is that it will help us get rid of the negative programming so that we may enjoy our menopause, instead of fearing it."

Shange, Ntozake, *Sassafrass, Cypress & Indigo.* New York: St. Martin's Press, 1982.

Sherfey, Mary Jane. *The Nature and Evolution of Female Sexuality.* New York: Random House, 1973.

Shuttle, Penelope and Peter Redgrove, *The Wise Wound.* New York: Richard Marek, 1978. An excellent book on the meaning of menstruation.

Thompson, William Irwin, *The Time Falling Bodies Take To Light.* New York: St. Martin's Press, 1981. Thompson's book is dedicated "To the Eternal Feminine: this research into Her epiphanies in the darkness of the past is a search in light of the future."

Walker, Barbara G., *The Women's Encyclopedia of Myths & Secrets.* San Francisco: Harper & Row, 1983.

Weideger, Paula, *Menstruation & Menopause.* New York: Alfred A. Knopf, Inc., 1975.

Wright, Ann L., "A Cross-Cultural Comparison of Menopausal Symptoms," *Medical Anthology,* 7, 2, 1983.

Notes

Introduction

1. Judy Grahn, "From Sacred Blood to the Curse and Beyond," *The Politics of Women's Spirituality* (N.Y.: Anchor Press, 1982), p. 272.
2. Barbara G. Walker, *The Women's Encyclopedia of Myths and Secrets* (San Francisco: Harper & Row, 1983), p. 638.
3. Ibid.
4. Grahn, op. cit., pp. 266-7.

Chapter 1: Menarche: First Blood

1. *Illustrated Heritage Dictionary*.
2. Jeanne Brooks-Gunn, "Developmental Processes in the Experience of Menarche," in *The Handbook of Medical Psychology: Issues in Child Health and Illness,* Ed. A. Baum and J.E. Singer, 1981, p. 8.
3. From Mary Beth Edelson's "Menstruation Stories."
4. Ibid.
5. Judy Grahn, op. cit., p. 276.
6. Jill Rierdan, Elissa Koff, Jenny Flaherty, "Preparation for Menstruation: Adolescents' Reflections and Advice," working paper #96, Wellesley College, MA, 1982, p. 4.
7. Emma Goldman, *Living My Life,* Vol. 1 (N.Y.: Dover Press, 1970), p. 21.
8. Mary Jane Sherfey, *The Nature & Evolution of Female Sexuality* (N.Y.: Random House, 1973), p. 12.
9. Ntozake Shange, *Sassafrass, Cypress & Indigo* (N.Y.: St. Martin's Press, 1982), pp. 19-21.
10. Bruce Lincoln, *Emerging from the Chrysalis* (Cambridge MA: Harvard University Press, 1981), pp. 17-33.
11. Ibid., pp. 34-49.
12. Colin N. Turnbull, *The Forest People* (Garden City, New York: Doubleday and Company, 1961), pp. 190-1.
13. Ruth Underhill, *The Navajos* (Norman, OK: Univ. of Oklahoma Press, 1956), pp. 8,10.
14. Claire Farrer, "Singing for Life: The Mescalero Apache Girls' Puberty Ceremony," *Betwixt & Between: Patterns of Masculine and Feminine Initiation,* Ed. Louise Mahdi, Steven Foster and Meredith Little (La Salle, IL: Open Court, 1987), pp. 240-262.
15. Alice J. Dan, "The Law and Women's Bodies: The Case of Menstruation Leave in Japan," *Culture, Society, and Menstruation,* Ed. Virginia L. Olesen and Nancy Fugate Woods (Washington: Hemisphere Publishing Corp., 1986), p. 7.
16. Janice Delaney, Mary Jane Lupton, and Emily Toth, *The Curse* (N.Y.: E.P. Dutton & Co., Inc., 1976), pp. 30-31.
17. Penelope Shuttle and Peter Redgrove, *The Wise Wound* (N.Y.: Richard Marek, 1978), p. 62.

18. Turnbull, op. cit., p. 189.
19. Marla N. Powers, "Menstruation and Reproduction: An Oglala Case," *Women—Sex & Sexuality,* Ed. Catherine Stimson and Ethel Person (Chicago: Univ. of Chicago Press, 1981), p. 120.
20. Lincoln, op. cit., p. ix.
21. Powers, op. cit., p. 119.
22. Karen Paige & Jeffery Paige, *The Politics of Reproductive Ritual* (Berkeley: Univ. of California Press, 1981), p. 20.
23. Lincoln, op. cit., p. 99.
24. Paige, op. cit., p. 8.
25. Lincoln, op. cit., p. 105.
26. Ibid., p. 107.
27. Ibid., p. 106.
28. Rierdan, op. cit., pp. 9-11.
29. Ibid., pp. 13-14.
30. Edelson's "Menstruation Stories."
31. Submitted by Penny Kemp.

Chapter 2: Seclusion and Power

1. *The Bible,* Leviticus 15:19-33.
2. Delaney, op. cit., p. 10, and Paula Weideger, *Menstruation & Menopause* (N.Y.: Alfred A. Knopf, Inc., 1975), p. 95.
3. Delaney, op. cit., p. 11.
4. Walker, op. cit., p. 644.
5. Ruby Rohrlich Leavitt, *Peaceable Primates and Gentle People: Anthropological Approaches to Women's Studies,* (N.Y.: Harper & Row, Inc., 1975) pp. 31-32.
6. R. Lowie quoted in Chris Knight, "Levi-Strauss and the Dragon: Mythologiques Reconsidered in the Light of an Australian Aboriginal Myth," *Man,* Vol. 18, 1983, p. 28.
7. Avodah K. Offit, M.D., *Night Thoughts - Reflections of a Sex Therapist* (N.Y.: Congdon & Lattes, Inc.), p. 51.
8. Knight, op. cit., p. 28.
9. Shuttle, op. cit., p. 218.
10. "Laws of Family Purity," *Torah Laws for the Modern Jewish Woman* (N.Y.: United Jewish Women for Taharas Hamishpocho, 1965), p. 42.
11. Margaret Mead, *Male and Female* (N.Y.: Morrow, 1949), p. 222.
12. Delaney, op. cit., p. 31.
13. Walker, op. cit., p. 620.
14. Ibid., p. 644.
15. Ibid., p. 641.
16. Vicki Noble, "Female Blood—Roots of Shamanism," *Shaman's Drum,* Spring 1986, p. 18.
17. Ruby Modesto and Guy Mount, *Not for Innocent Ears* (Arcata, CA: Sweetlight Books, 1980), p. 42.
18. Thomas Buckley, "Menstruation and the power of Yurok women: methods of cultural reconstruction," *American Ethnologist,* 9, pp. 47-60.
19. Knight, op. cit., pp. 27-8.
20. Shuttle, op. cit., p. 166.
21. Ibid., p. 184.
22. Ibid.

23. Carolyn Berry, "Indian Women and Menstruation," unpublished article.
24. William Irwin Thompson, *The Time Falling Bodies Take To Light* (N.Y.: St. Martin's Press, 1981), p. 97.
25. Grahn, op. cit., pp. 268-9.
26. Shuttle, op. cit., pp. 134-5.
27. Noble, op. cit., pp. 18-19.
28. Dan, op. cit., pp. 1-14.

Chapter 3: Dreamtime

1. Shuttle, op. cit., p. 96.
2. Ibid.
3. Marilyn Nagy, "Menstruation and Shamanism," *Betwixt and Between*, op. cit., pp. 228-9.
4. Shuttle, op. cit., p. 100.
5. Ibid., p. 97.
6. Ibid., p. 96.
7. Ibid., p. 97.
8. Ibid., p. 174.
9. Ibid., p. 123.
10. Michelle Cliff, *Abeng* (N.Y.: The Crossing Press, 1984), p. 165.
11. Hilary C. Maddux, *Menstruation* (New Canaan, Conn: Tokey Pub. Co., 1975).
12. Brooke Medicine Eagle, "Women's Moontime—A Call to Power," *Shaman's Drum*, op. cit., p. 24.

Chapter 4: The Sexuality of Menstruation

1. Nagy, op. cit., p. 231.
2. Comments from Questionnaire.
3. Weideger, op. cit., p. 125.
4. Ibid.
5. Walker, op. cit., p. 641.
6. Ibid., p. 638.
7. Shuttle, op. cit., p. 88.
8. Sherfey, op. cit., p. 96.
9. Shuttle, op. cit., p. 89.
10. Sherfey, op. cit., p. 97.
11. Ibid.
12. Comment from questionnaire.
13. Shuttle, op. cit., p. 142.
14. Comment from questionnaire.
15. Noble, op. cit., p. 19.
16. Shuttle, op. cit., p. 33.
17. Ibid., p. 96.
18. Sherfey, op. cit., p. 52.
19. Ann Mankowitz, *Change of Life* (Toronto, Canada: Inner City Books, 1984), pp. 22-3.
20. Shuttle, op. cit., p. 92.

Chapter 5: Menstruation and Men

1. Comment from questionnaire.
2. Walker, op. cit., p. 638.
3. Philip Roth, *Portnoy's Complaint* (N.Y.: Random House, 1969), cited in Rosetta Reitz, *Menopause—A Positive Approach* (N.Y.: Penguin, 1977), p. 84.
4. Grahn, op. cit., p. 272.
5. Thompson, op. cit., p. 99.
6. Shuttle, op. cit., p. 67.
7. Grahn, op. cit., p. 273.
8. Weideger, op. cit., p. 107.
9. Grahn, op. cit., p. 274.
10. Phyllis Chesler, *About Men* (N.Y.: Bantam Books, 1978), p. xx.
11. Shuttle, op. cit., p. 68.
12. Knight, op. cit., pp. 32, 43.
13. Paige, op. cit., pp. 28-9.
14. Grahn, op. cit., p. 275.
15. Ibid.

Chapter 6: Pain and PMS

1. Sophie Laws, Valerie Hey and Andrea Eagan, *Seeing Red* (London: Hutchinson & Co. Ltd., 1985), p. 37.
2. "PMS Food Alert," *Redbook*, Feb. 1984, p. 10.
3. Janet Hopson and Anne Rosenfeld, "PMS: Puzzling Monthly Symptoms," *Psychology Today*, Aug. 1984, pp. 30-35.
4. Shuttle, op. cit., p. 51.
5. Judy Lever, *Pre-Menstrual Tension* (N.Y.: McGraw-Hill Book Co., 1981), xii.
6. Reitz, op. cit., pp. 68-9.
7. Laws, op. cit., p. 41.
8. Reitz, op. cit. pp. 68-9.
9. Lever, op. cit., p. 54.
10. An extreme example of disgust with menstruation and women's bodies in general is found in women who suffer with anorexia nervosa, whose bodies are so thin that menstruation stops. Ninety percent of anorexics are women, who in this culture are told by the media that large women are not attractive. See Susan Bordo, "Anorexia Nervosa: psychopathology as the crystalization of culture," in *Feminism and Foucault*, Ed. I. Diamond and L. Quinby (Boston: Northeastern University Press, 1988), p. 102.
11. Laws, op. cit., p. 42.
12. Hopson, op. cit.
13. Laws, op. cit., 42.
14. Weideger, op. cit., p. 204.
15. Ibid., p. 146.
16. Laws, op. ct., p. 86.
17. Shainess' study cited in Lever, op. cit., p. 162.
18. Laws, op. cit., p. 58.
19. For an excellent discussion of this point of view, see "Who Needs PMT? A feminist approach to the politics of premenstrual tension," by Sophie Laws in *Seeing Red*, op. cit., pp 16-64.

20. "PMS Food Alert," *Redbook*, op. cit.
21. Grahn, op. cit., p. 277.
22. "Remedies for Menstrual Problems" by the Boston Women's Health Book Collective, compiled by Esther Rome and Emily Culpepper, 1977.
23. Comments from questionnaire.
24. Laws, op. cit., p. 88.
25. Dr. Gary Shangold of the Univ. of Chicago, reported in *The Santa Cruz Sentinel*, Jan. 8, 1985.
26. Day and Taylor, 1981, cited in Laws, op. cit., p. 48.
27. Laws, Ibid., p. 31.
28. Ibid., pp. 83-4.
29. Ibid., p. 35.
30. Ibid., pp. 84, 86-7.
31. Ibid., pp. 83-4.
32. Ibid., p. 47.
33. Ibid., p. 47.
34. Penny Wise Budhoff, *No More Menstrual Cramps and Other Good News* (N.Y.: Penguin Books, 1980), pp. 59-60.
35. "The pre-curse threatens women again" by Ellen Goodman, *Santa Cruz Sentinel*, May 25, 1986.
36. Laws, op. cit., p. 65.
37. Ibid., p. 11.
38. Goodman, op. cit.
39. Laws, op. cit., p. 13.
40. Nadine Brozan, "Premenstrual Syndrome: A Complex Issue," *New York Times*, July 12, 1982.
41. Goodman, op. cit.
42. Laws, op. cit., pp. 12, 76.
43. Ibid., p. 35.
44. Ibid., p. 42.
45. Ibid., p. 45.
46. Susan Brownmiller, *Femininity* (N.Y.: Simon & Shuster, 1984), pp. 193-4.
47. Hopson, op. cit., p. 35.
48. Grahn, op. cit., pp. 277-8.
49. Lynda Birke & Katy Gardner, *Why Suffer?* (London: Virago, 1979), p. 33.
50. Laws, op. cit., p. 35.
51. Shuttle, op. cit., p. 41.

Chapter 7: Menstrual Blood

1. Walker, op. cit., pp. 636, 639.
2. Lederer, quoted in Walker, ibid., p. 636.
3. Walker, ibid., p. 636.
4. Ibid., p. 635.
5. Comment from questionnaire.
6. Comments from questionnaire.
7. Delaney, op. cit., pp. 241-2.
8. Carolyn Berry, "Celebrating the Blood: Indian Women and Menstruation," *Bread and Roses*, Vol. 3, No. 2, 1984, p. 16.

9. Nancy Friedman, *Everything You Must Know About Tampons* (N.Y.: Berkley Books, 1981), p. 34.
10. V.L. Oleson, "Analyzing Emergent Issues in Women's Health: The Case of the Toxic-Shock Syndrome," *Culture, Society, and Menstruation,* op. cit., p. 52.
11. Freidman, op. cit., p. 5; these are 1981 figures.
12. Ibid., p. 160.
13. Ibid., pp. 4-5.
14. Ibid., p. 52.
15. *Mademoiselle,* Sept. 1986, p. 166.
16. Friedman, op. cit., pp. 55, 66-8.
17. Ibid., pp. 5-6.
18. Ibid., p. 54.
19. *Journal of the American Medical Association,* Aug. 21, 1987, p. 917.
20. Boston Women's Health Book Collective handout, 1986.
21. Friedman, op. cit. pp. x, xi.
22. Ibid., pp. 10, 154-6, and BWHBC handout. The Coalition for the Medical Rights of Women urges women to report any problems they have with tampons to the FDA to this address:

    DEN (Device Experience Network) Reports
    Food and Drug Administration
    5600 Fishers Lane
    Rockville, MD 20857

    Women should also send copies of letters to:

    The Boston Women's Health Book Collective
    P.O. Box 192
    W. Somerville, MA 02144

    Problems that should be reported are vaginal sores, allergic reactions, irritation, unusual bleeding, infections, fragmentation, foreign material in tampons, and injuries from inserters. The Coalition says: "All you have to do is write a letter including your name and address (which are kept confidential), the brand and type of tampon, and the problem(s) you experienced. Even if you received medical treatment, send in a report yourself. Most medical practitioners do not know about DEN reports or do not bother to report problems with tampons." (*Second Opinion,* The Coalition for the Medical Rights of Women, Feb. 1984, p. 2).

    Both the Coalition and the Boston Women's Health Collective urge women to write to Mr. John Villforth at the FDA (same address as above) asking for absorbency labeling on tampon boxes.
23. Friedman, op. cit., p. 152.
24. Jeannine Parvati, *Hygieia* (Monroe, Utah: Freestone Publishing Co., 1978), p. 14.
25. Friedman, op. cit., pp. 135-6.
26. Ibid., p. 94.
27. Ibid., pp. 137-8.
28. "Menstruation," a handout from the BWHBC, compiled by Esther Rome and Emily Culpepper, 1977.
29. "using a menstrual sponge," unpublished manuscript by zana.
30. Parvati, op. cit, p. 13.
31. Ibid., p. 14.
32. Ibid., p. 15.
33. Comments from questionnaire.
34. "Menstruation," handout published by the Boston Women's Health Book Collective.
35. Friedman, op. cit., pp. 140-4.
36. From Mary Beth Edelson's collection of "Menstruation Stories."

37. Delaney, op. cit., p. 215.
38. Ibid., pp. 118, 216.
39. Nora Ephron, *Crazy Salad* (N.Y.: Bantam Books, 1976), p. 49.

Chapter 8: Menopause: Last Blood

1. Pauline Bart, "Menopause," *Women and Health,* May/June, 1976, pp. 3-11.
2. Reitz, op. cit. p. 107.
3. Ibid., pp. 7, 194.
4. Ibid., p. 4.
5. Weideger, op. cit., p. 53.
6. Chesler, op. cit., p. xx.
7. Philip Slater, *Earthwalk* (N.Y.: Anchor, 1974), p. 155.
8. Reitz, op. cit., p. 17.
9. Ibid., p. 18.
10. Ibid., p. 15.
11. Ibid., pp. 15-16, 160.
12. Ibid., p. 171.
13. Ibid., pp. 19-20.
14. Ibid., pp. 21, 25.
15. Ibid., p. 26.
16. Ibid., pp. 29-31.
17. Barbara Raskin, *Hot Flashes* (N.Y.: St. Martin's Press, 1987), p. 2.
18. Ibid., p. 3.
19. Ibid.
20. Louisa Rose, *Menopause Book* (N.Y.: Hawthorne Books, Inc., 1977), pp. 16-17.
21. Phyllis Chesler, *Women and Madness* (N.Y.: Avon Books, 1972), cited in Reitz, op. cit., p. 65.
22. Reitz, op. cit., p. 67.
23. Susan E. Brown, from a forthcoming book, *Osteoporosis in Anthropological Perspective.*
24. Ibid.
25. Ibid.
26. Ibid.
27. Reitz, op. cit., p. 36.
28. Ibid., p. 107.
29. Ibid., throughout.
30. Ibid., pp. 22-24.
31. Ibid., p. 74.
32. Ibid., pp. 27-8.
33. Morris Notelovitz and Marsha Ware, *Stand Tall* (New York: Bantam Books, 1985), pp. 120-3.
34. Reitz, op. cit., p. 159.
35. Ibid., pp. 167-9.
36. Ibid., pp. 178-185.
37. See, for example, Bruce E. Hinger, "Overview of the efficacy of hormonal replacement therapy," *American Journal of Obstetrics and Gynecology* 87 May 156(5):1298-1303.
38. Brown, op. cit.
39. Ibid.
40. Paige, op. cit., pp. 211-2.

41. Marcha Flint, "The Menopause: Reward or Punishment?" in *Psychosomatics,* Vol. 16, pp. 161-3, Fourth Quarter 1975.
42. Bart, op. cit.
43. Ann L. Wright, "A Cross-Cultural Comparison of Menopausal Symptoms," *Medical Anthology:* 7,2,1983, pp. 27-8.
44. Brown, op. cit.
45. Nancy Rosenberger, "Menopause as a Symbol of Anomaly: The Case of Japanese Women," in *Culture, Society, & Menstruation,* op. cit., pp. 16-18.
46. Ibid., p. 23.
47. Walker, op. cit., p. 641.
48. Joan B. Forest, "Honoring Our Passage," in *Matrix,* Dec. 1986.
49. Reitz, op. cit., p. 114.

Epilogue

1. Comment from questionnaire.
2. Parvati, op. cit., p. 10.

Index

About the Author

Dena Taylor, M.S.W., is a freelance writer and researcher. She is the co-editor of *Women of the 14th Moon: Writings on Menopause* (1991) and *Sexual Harassment: Women Speak Out* (1992). She lives with her two teenage daughters in Capitola, CA.